Idioms and Phrases

Perfecting Expressions in English

READERS CHOICE

New Delhi - 110002

Idioms and Phrases

Perfecting Expressions in English

Ajay Sharma

READERS CHOICE
New Delhi - 110002

Idioms and Phrases

Perfecting Expressions in English

ISBN 978-81-922292-4-9

Published by:

Readers Choice

103, 4787/23, Ansari Road,
Daryaganj, New Delhi - 110002
Ph: 9654444181

Laser typesetting by: Naissance Books, New Delhi.
Printed at: Navprabhat Printing Press, Delhi

Preface

Idioms are one of the most colourful and fascinating aspects of a language. They are commonly used in all types of language, written and spoken.

Idioms also suggest a particular attitude of the person using them, for example disapproval, humour, exasperation, respect or admiration, so they must be used carefully, to not to make people misunderstand or understand you incorrectly.

People often use idioms in order to create a sense of 'camaraderie' with the people they are speaking to or writing for: idioms make language seem more lively and interesting, friendlier and more informal.

For example, look at the following sentence:

'Hello the man not familiar to me!'

Recognize it? It might sound a somewhat mangled version of 'Hello stranger!'. However, it doesn't have the same impact somehow, does it?

Because of such features, idioms are generally considered informal. In fact, idioms are often used in contexts which are not informal at all. That is why idioms should be used attentively, in other case they may be interpreted as critical or disapproving, and therefore unintentionally cause the wrong reaction.

Also, idioms are used to give emphasis or to organize speech, to paraphrase what is going on, and what is being said. Idioms help language learners understand English culture, traditions, lifestyle of English people and make a deeper insight to English history.

Idioms make a language more interesting and vibrant. Mastering idioms can denote that the user is using and understanding the language more like a native speaker would.

Nonetheless, the tough part about mastering idioms is that knowing all the individual words may not help you to understand the meaning of the phrase. For example, knowing the meanings of ace and hole may not help you to understand the meaning of 'An ace in the hole'.

To help the readers understand and become able to use idioms fluently, the present book is written with the most direct and simple approach. Hope the effort of the writer is helpful and acknowledged.

–Author

Contents

1

What are Idioms and Phrases?

An idiom is an expression, word, or phrase that has a figurative meaning that is comprehended in regard to a common use of that expression that is separate from the literal meaning or definition of the words of which it is made.

In English language, there are estimated to be at least 25,000 idiomatic expressions and phrases. Usually, an idiom's meaning is not deducible and does not have an analogue in others languages so it often is quite difficult for non-native speakers, especially ones who are not good at the language, to understand and to use them properly. Nevertheless, many idioms have their equivalents in other languages. In some cases, it is fairly easy to see how the idiomatic meaning relates to the literal meaning. For example, kill two birds with one stone means 'to achieve two things at the same time', and the image in the metaphor supports the meaning. Another example is 'fine and dandy', what means that everything is going well. In other cases, the literal meaning does not make sense at all. For example, to go for an early bath means 'to lose a job or a position because things have gone wrong'. The best way to understand an idiom without using a dictionary is to see it in context. If someone says: He owns some old iron mines that have not been used in donkey's ears, then listener, using the context and common sense understands the meaning 'to last for a very long time'.

Types of Idioms

There are several types of idioms, which are differently formed. Here are some with examples:

Whole clause or sentence:

- To sort out the men from the boys (a difficult or challenging situation tests people and shows who is strong and capable and who is not)
- A millstone around your neck (a very unpleasant problem or responsibility that you cannot escape from)
- To give someone a piece of your mind (someone has annoyed or upset you and you angrily tell them what do you think of them)

Prepositional phrase:

- In your mind's eye (to have a clear picture of something in your imagination or memory)
- On the nail (to pay for something immediately and in cash)
- On the nod (something is accepted without being questioned or argued)

Verb + object/complement (and/or adverbial):

- To keep your nose clean (to behave well and avoid trouble)
- To go nuclear (to get extremely angry and start behaving in a forceful or irrational way as a result)
- To turn the page (to make a fresh start after a period of difficulties and troubles)

Compound:

- Growing pains (temporary difficulties and problems as it develops and grows stronger)
- A paper tiger (a person, country, or organization that seems to be powerful and actually does not have any power)

- A close shave (someone was very nearly to have a disaster or an accident, or very nearly suffered a defeat)

Simile (as + adjective + as/like + noun):

- Nice as pie (a very kind, friendly, charming person)
- Nutty as a fruitcake (a strange, foolish or crazy person)
- Old as the hills (something very old, and perhaps old-fashioned or very traditional)

Binomial (word + and + word):

- A nod and a wink (someone communicates indirectly or by giving some kind of signal)
- Neck and neck (two competitors are exactly level with each other, so that it is impossible to say who will win)
- Oil and water (two people or things are very different and they cannot work together or exist together successfully)

Trinomial (word + word + and + word):

- Signed, sealed and delivered (an agreement is official and cannot be changed)
- Every Tom, Dick and Harry (ordinary people who do not have any special skills or qualities)
- Cool, calm and collected (relaxed, in control, not nervous)

Exclamation or saying:

- Act your age! (Something that you say to someone who is being silly to tell them to behave in a more serious way)
- Over my dead body! (Someone is going to do everything to prevent something)
- Bully for you! (Something that you say when you do not think what someone has done deserves praise or admiration, although they think it does)

❖❖❖

2

List of Idioms and Phrases

A

- **A bit much**

  Meaning: If something is excessive or annoying, it is a bit much.
- **A bridge too far**

  Meaning: A bridge too far is an act of overreaching– going too far and getting into trouble or failing.
- **A chain is no stronger than its weakest link**

  Meaning: This means that processes, organizations, etc., are vulnerable because the weakest person or part can always damage or break them.
- **A fool at 40 is a fool forever**

  Meaning: If someone hasn't matured by the time they reach forty, they never will.
- **A fresh pair of eyes**

  Meaning: A person who is brought in to examine something carefully is a fresh pair of eyes.

- **A hitch in your giddy-up**
  Meaning: If you have a hitch in your giddy-up, you're not feeling well.
- **A lick and a promise**
  Meaning: If you give something a lick and a promise, you do it hurriedly, most often incompletely, intending to return to it later.
- **A List**
  Meaning: Prominent and influential people who comprise the most desirable guests at a social function or gathering.
- **A little bird told me**
  Meaning: If someone doesn't want to say where they got some information from, they can say that a little bird told them.
- **A long row to hoe**
  Meaning: Something that is a long row to hoe is a difficult task that takes a long time.
- **A lost ball in the high weeds**
  Meaning: A lost ball in the high weeds is someone who does not know what they are doing, where they are or how to do something.
- **A lot on my plate**
  Meaning: If you have got a lot on your plate, you are very busy and have commitments.
- **A month of Sundays**
  Meaning: A month of Sundays is a long period of time: I haven't seen her in a month of Sundays.
- **A OK**
  Meaning: If things are A OK, they are absolutely fine.
- **A penny for your thoughts**
  Meaning: This idiom is used as a way of asking someone what they are thinking about.
- **A penny saved is a penny earned**
  Meaning: Saving money is just as important as earning money– we shouldn't spend it foolishly.

- **A picture is worth a thousand words**

  Meaning: A picture can often get a message across much better than the best verbal description.

- **A poor man's something**

  Meaning: Something or someone that can be compared to something or someone else, but is not as good is a poor man's version.

- **A pretty penny**

  Meaning: If something costs a pretty penny, it is very expensive.

- **A problem shared is a problem halved**

  Meaning: If you talk about your problems, it will make you feel better.

- **A rising tide lifts all boats**

  Meaning: This idiom, describes the idea that when an economy is performing well, all people will benefit from it.

- **A shallow brook babbles the loudest**

  Meaning: People who are loud and talk a lot usually have nothing of substance to say.

- **A steal**

  Meaning: If something is a steal, it costs much less than it is really worth.

- **A still tongue keeps a wise head**

  Meaning: Wise people don't talk much.

- **A textbook case**

  Meaning: A textbook case, it is a classic or common example of something.

- **A watched pot never boils**

  Meaning: Some things work out in their own time, so being impatient and constantly checking will just make things seem longer.

- **A1**

  Meaning: If something is A1, it is the very best or finest.

- **ABC**

  Meaning: ABC means the basics of something– knowing the ABC of science, etc.
- **Abide by a decision**

  Meaning: If you abide by a decision, you accept it and comply with it, even though you might disagree with it.
- **Abject lesson**

  Meaning: An abject lesson serves as a warning to others.
- **About as useful as a chocolate teapot**

  Meaning: Someone or something that is of no practical use is about as useful as a chocolate teapot.
- **Above board**

  Meaning: If things are done above board, they are carried out in a legal and proper manner.
- **Above par**

  Meaning: Better than average or normal.
- **Above the salt**

  Meaning: This means that something or someone has a high position.
- **Absence makes the heart grow fonder**

  Meaning: This idiom means that when people are apart, their love grows stronger.
- **Ace in the hole**

  Meaning: An ace in the hole is something other people are not aware of that can be used to your advantage when the time is right.
- **Ace up your sleeve**

  Meaning: If you have an acc up your sleeve, you have something that will give you an advantage that other people don't know about.
- **Achilles' heel**

  Meaning: A person's weak spot is their Achilles' heel.

- **Acid test**

  Meaning: An acid test is something that proves whether something is good, effective, etc., or not.

- **Across the board**

  Meaning: If something applies to everybody, it applies across the board.

- **Act of God**

  Meaning: An act of God is something like an earthquake or floods that human beings cannot prevent or control.

- **Act of war**

  Meaning: An act of war is an action that is either intended to start a war or that is interpreted as being sufficient cause for a war.

- **Actions speak louder than words**

  Meaning: This idiom means that what people actually do is more important than what they say- people can promise things but then fail to deliver.

- **Add fuel to the fire**

  Meaning: If people add fuel to the fire, they make a bad situation worse.

- **Add insult to injury**

  Meaning: When people add insult to injury, they make a bad situation even worse.

- **After your own heart**

  Meaning: A person after your own heart thinks the same way as you.

- **Against the clock**

  Meaning: If you do something against the clock, you are rushed and have very little time to do it.

- **Against the grain**

  Meaning: If doing something goes against the grain, you're unwilling to do it because it contradicts what you believe in, but you have no real choice.

- **Age before beauty**

  Meaning: When this idiom is used, it is a way of allowing an older person to do something first, though often in a slightly sarcastic way.

- **Agony aunt**

  Meaning: An agony aunt is a newspaper columnist who gives advice to people having problems, especially personal ones.

- **Ahead of the pack**

  Meaning: If you are ahead of the pack, you have made more progress than your rivals.

- **Ahead of time**

  Meaning: If something happens ahead of time, it happens early or before the set time.

- **Albatross around your neck**

  Meaning: An albatross around, or round, your neck is a problem resulting from something you did that stops you from being successful.

- **Alike as two peas**

  Meaning: Identical people, things or events.

- **Alive and kicking**

  Meaning: If something is active and doing well, it is alive and kicking.

- **All ages and stripes**

  Meaning: Shorthand for expressing a diversity of folks in a group.

- **All along**

  Meaning: If you have known or suspected something all along, then you have felt this from the beginning.

- **All and sundry**

  Meaning: This idiom is a way of emphasizing 'all', like saying 'each and every one'.

- **All bark and no bite**

  Meaning: When someone talks tough but really isn't, they are all bark and no bite.

- **All bets are off**

  Meaning: If all bets are off, then agreements that have been made no longer apply.

- **All cats are grey in the dark**

  Meaning: Things are indistinguishable in the dark so appearances don't matter.

- **All dressed up and nowhere to go**

  Meaning: You're prepared for something that isn't going to happen.

- **All ears**

  Meaning: If someone says they're all ears, they are very interested in hearing about something.

- **All eyes on me**

  Meaning: If all eyes are on someone, then everyone is paying attention to them.

- **All hat, no cattle**

  Meaning: When someone talks big, but cannot back it up, they are all hat, no cattle.

- **All heart**

  Meaning: Someone who is all heart is very kind and generous.

- **All hell broke loose**

  Meaning: When all hell breaks loose, there is chaos, confusion and trouble.

- **All in a day's work**

  Meaning: If something is all in a day's work, it is nothing special.

- **All in your head**

  Meaning: Something imagined and not real.

- **All of the above**

  Meaning: This idiom can be used to mean everything that has been said or written, especially all the choices or possibilities.

- **All over bar the shouting**

  Meaning: When something is all over bar the shouting, the outcome is absolutely certain.

- **All over the map**

  Meaning: If something like a discussion is all over the map, it doesn't stick to the main topic and goes off on tangents.
- **All over the place**

  Meaning: If something is completely disorganized or confused, it is all over the place.
- **All over the shop**

  Meaning: If something is completely disorganized or confused, it is all over the shop.
- **All over the show**

  Meaning: If something is all over the show, it's in a complete mess.
- **All roads lead to Rome**

  Meaning: This means that there can be many different ways of doing something.
- **All set**

  Meaning: If you're all set, you are ready for something.
- **All sixes**

  Meaning: If something is all sixes, it doesn't matter how it's done; it's the same as 'six of one and half a dozen of the other'.
- **All skin and bone**

  Meaning: If a person is very underweight, they are all skin and bone, or bones.
- **All square**

  Meaning: If something is all square, nobody has an advantage or is ahead of the others.
- **All talk and no trousers**

  Meaning: Someone who is all talk and no trousers, talks about doing big, important things, but doesn't take any action.
- **All the rage**

  Meaning: If something's all the rage, it is very popular or fashionable at the moment.
- **All the tea in China**

  Meaning: If someone won't do something for all the tea in

China, they won't do it no matter how much money they are offered.

- **All's fair in love and war**

  Meaning: This idiom is used to say that where there is conflict people can be expected to behave in a more vicious way.

- **All's well that ends well**

  Meaning: If the end result is good, then everything is good.

- **All-singing, all-dancing**

  Meaning: If something's all-singing, all-dancing, it is the latest version with the most up-to-date features.

- **Alter ego**

  Meaning: An alter ego is a very close and intimate friend. It is a Latin phrase that literally means 'other self'.

- **Ambulance chaser**

  Meaning: A lawyer who encourages people who have been in accidents or become ill to sue for compensation is an ambulance chaser.

- **Amen**

  Meaning: Some use 'Amen' or 'Amen to that' as a way of agreeing with something that has just been said.

- **An apple a day keeps the doctor away**

  Meaning: Eating healthy food keeps you healthy.

- **An Englishman's home is his castle**

  Meaning: This means that what happens in a person's home or private life is their business and should not be subject to outside interference.

- **An old flame**

  Meaning: An old flame is a person that somebody has had an emotional, usually passionate, relationship with, who is still looked on fondly and with affection.

- **An ounce of prevention is worth a pound of cure**

  Meaning: This expression means that it is better to try to avoid problems in the first place, rather than trying to fix them once they arise.

- **And all that jazz**

  Meaning: This idiom means that everything related or similar is included.
- **Angry as a bear**

  Meaning: If someone is as angry as a bear, they are very angry.
- **Angry as a bull**

  Meaning: If someone is as angry as a bull, they are very angry.
- **Answers on a postcard**

  Meaning: This idiom can be used to suggest that the answer to something is very obvious or that the person would really like to hear what people think.
- **Ants in your pants**

  Meaning: If someone has ants in their pants, they are agitated or excited about something and can't keep still.
- **Any port in a storm**

  Meaning: This means that in an emergency any solution will do, even one that would normally be unacceptable.
- **Any Tom, Dick or Harry**

  Meaning: If something could be done by any Tom, Dick or Harry, it could be done by absolutely anyone.
- **Apple of your eye**

  Meaning: Something or, more often, someone that is very special to you is the 'apple of your' eye.
- **Apple pie order**

  Meaning: Everything is in perfect order and tidy if it is in apple pie order.
- **Apples and oranges**

  Meaning: 'Apples and oranges' used when people compare or describe two totally different things.
- **Apples for apples**

  Meaning: Denotes comparison between related or similar things.
- **Apron strings**

  Meaning: A man who is tied to a woman's apron strings is excessively dependent on her, especially when it is his mother's apron strings.

- **Argue the toss**

  Meaning: If you argue the toss, you refuse to accept a decision and argue about it.
- **Arm and a leg**

  Meaning: If something costs an arm and a leg, it is very expensive.
- **Armchair critic**

  Meaning: An armchair critic is someone who offers advice but never shows that they could actually do any better.
- **Armchair quarterback**

  Meaning: An armchair quarterback is someone who offers advice, especially about football, but never shows that they could actually do any better.
- **Armed to the teeth**

  Meaning: If people are armed to the teeth, they have lots of weapons.
- **Around the clock**

  Meaning: If something is open around the clock, it is open 24 hours a day. For example, an airport is open around the clock.
- **Arrow in the quiver**

  Meaning: An arrow in the quiver is a strategy or option that could be used to achieve your objective.
- **As a rule**

  Meaning: If you do something as a rule, then you usually do it.
- **As cold as ice**

  Meaning: This idiom can be used to describe a person who does not show any emotion.
- **As cold as stone**

  Meaning: If something is as cold as stone, it is very cold. If a person is as cold as stone, they are unemotional.
- **As cool as a cucumber**

  Meaning: If someone is as cool as a cucumber, they don't get worried by anything.

- **As good as new**

  Meaning: If something has been used but is still in extremely good condition, it is as good as new.

- **As mad as a hatter**

  Meaning: It means that someone is crazy or behaves very strangely.

- **As mad as a wrongly shot hog**

  Meaning: If someone is as mad as a wrongly shot hog, they are very angry.

- **As much use as a chocolate fire-guard**

  Meaning: A fire-guard is used in front of a fireplace for safety. A chocolate fire-guard is of no use.

- **As much use as a chocolate teapot**

  Meaning: Something that is as much use as a chocolate teapot is not useful at all.

- **As much use as a handbrake on a canoe**

  Meaning: This idiom is used to describe someone or something as worthless or pointless.

- **As neat as a new pin**

  Meaning: This idiom means tidy and clean.

- **As one man**

  Meaning: If people do something as one man, then they do it at exactly the same time or in complete agreement.

- **As rare as hen's teeth**

  Meaning: Something that is rare as hen's teeth is very rare or non-existent.

- **As the crow flies**

  Meaning: This idiom is used to describe the shortest possible distance between two places.

- **As you sow, so shall you reap**

  Meaning: This means that if you do bad things to people, bad things will happen to you, or good things if you do good things.

- **Asleep at the switch**

  Meaning: If someone is asleep at the switch, they are not doing their job or taking their responsibilities very carefully.

- **At a drop of a dime**

  Meaning: If someone will do something at the drop of a dime, they will do it instantly, without hesitation.

- **At a loose end**

  Meaning: If you are at a loose end, you have spare time but don't know what to do with it.

- **At a loss**

  Meaning: If you are at a loss, you are unable to understand or comply.

- **At a snail's pace**

  Meaning: If something moves at a snail's pace, it moves very slowly.

- **At arm's length**

  Meaning: If something is at arm's length, it is a safe distance away from you.

- **At cross purposes**

  Meaning: When people are at cross purposes, they misunderstand each other or have different or opposing objectives.

- **At daggers drawn**

  Meaning: If people are at daggers drawn, they are very angry and close to violence.

- **At death's door**

  Meaning: If someone looks as if they are at death's door, they look seriously unwell and might actually be dying.

- **At each other's throats**

  Meaning: If people are at each other's throats, they are fighting, arguing or competing ruthlessly.

- **At large**

  Meaning: If a criminal is at large, they have not been found or caught.

- **At loggerheads**

  Meaning: If people are at loggerheads, they are arguing and can't agree on anything.

- **At loose ends**

  Meaning: If you are at a loose end, you have spare time but don't know what to do with it.

- **At odds**

  Meaning: If you are at odds with someone, you cannot agree with them and argue.

- **At sea**

  Meaning: If things are at sea, or all at sea, they are disorganized and chaotic.

- **At the bottom of the totem pole**

  Meaning: If someone is at the bottom of the totem pole, they are unimportant.

- **At the coalface**

  Meaning: If you work at the coalface, you deal with the real problems and issues, rather than sitting in an office discussing things in a detached way.

- **At the drop of a hat**

  Meaning: If you would do something at the drop of a hat, you'd do it immediately.

- **At the end of the day**

  Meaning: This is used to mean 'in conclusion' or 'when all is said and done'.

- **At the end of your rope**

  Meaning: If you are at the end of your rope, you are at the limit of your patience or endurance.

- **At the end of your tether**

  Meaning: If you are at the end of your tether, you are at the limit of your patience or endurance.

- **At the fore**

  Meaning: In a leading position.

- **At the top of my lungs**

  Meaning: If you shout at the top of your lungs, you shout as loudly as you possibly can.
- **At the top of the list**

  Meaning: If something is at the top of the list, it is of highest priority, most important, most urgent, or the next in one's line of attention.
- **At the top of your lungs**

  Meaning: If you shout at the top of your lungs, you shout as loudly as you possibly can.
- **At the top of your voice**

  Meaning: If you talk, shout or sing at the top of your voice, you do it as loudly as you can.
- **At your wits' end**

  Meaning: If you are at your wits' end, you have no idea what to do next and are very frustrated.
- **Average Joe**

  Meaning: An average Joe is an ordinary person without anything exceptional about them.
- **Avowed intent**

  Meaning: If someone makes a solemn or serious promise publicly to attempt to reach a certain goal, this is their avowed intent.
- **Away with the fairies**

  Meaning: If someone is away with the fairies, they don't face reality and have unrealistic expectations of life.
- **Awe inspiring**

  Meaning: Something or someone that is awe inspiring amazes people in a slightly frightening but positive way.
- **Axe to grind**

  Meaning: If you have an axe to grind with someone or about something, you have a grievance or resentment and you want to get revenge or sort it out.

B

- **Babe in arms**

  Meaning: A babe in arms is a very young child, or a person who is very young to be holding a position.
- **Babe in the woods**

  Meaning: A babe in the woods is a naive, defenceless, young person.
- **Back burner**

  Meaning: If an issue is on the back burner, it is being given low priority.
- **Back foot**

  Meaning: If you are on your back foot, you are at a disadvantage and forced to be defensive of your position.
- **Back number**

  Meaning: Something that's a back number is dated or out of fashion.
- **Back the wrong horse**

  Meaning: If you back the wrong horse, you give your support to the losing side in something.
- **Back to back**

  Meaning: If things happen back to back, they are directly one after another.
- **Back to square one**

  Meaning: If you are back to square one, you have to start from the beginning again.
- **Back to the drawing board**

  Meaning: If you have to go back to the drawing board, you have to go back to the beginning and start something again.
- **Back to the salt mines**

  Meaning: If someone says they have to go back to the salt mines, they have to return, possibly unwillingly, to work.
- **Back to the wall**

  Meaning: If you have your back to the wall, you are in a difficult situation with very little room for manoeuvre.

- **Bad Apple**
  Meaning: A person who is bad and makes other bad is a bad apple.
- **Bad blood**
  Meaning: If people feel hate because of things that happened in the past, there is bad blood between them.
- **Bad egg**
  Meaning: A person who cannot be trusted is a bad egg.
- **Bad hair day**
  Meaning: If you're having a bad hair day, things are not going the way you would like or had planned.
- **Bad mouth**
  Meaning: When you are bad mouthing, you are saying negative things about someone or something.
- **Bad shape**
  Meaning: If something's in bad shape, it's in bad condition. If a person's in bad shape, they are unfit or unhealthy.
- **Bad taste in your mouth**
  Meaning: If something leaves you with a bad taste in your mouth, you feel there is something wrong or bad about it.
- **Bag and baggage**
  Meaning: Bag and baggage means all your possessions, especially if you are moving them or leaving a place.
- **Bag of bones**
  Meaning: If someone is a bag of bones, they are very underweight.
- **Bag of nerves**
  Meaning: If someone is a bag of nerves, they are very worried or nervous.
- **Baker's dozen**
  Meaning: A Baker's dozen is 13 rather than 12.
- **Bald as a coot**
  Meaning: A person who is completely bald is as bald as a coot.

- **Ball is in your court**

  Meaning: If the ball is in your court, it is up to you to make the next decision or step.
- **Balloon goes up**

  Meaning: When the balloon goes up, a situation turns unpleasant or serious.
- **Balls to the walls**

  Meaning: If you do something balls to the wall, you apply full acceleration or exertion.
- **Banana republic**

  Meaning: Banana republic is a term used for small countries that are dependent on a single crop or resource and governed badly by a corrupt elite.
- **Banana skin**

  Meaning: A banana skin is something that is an embarrassment or causes problems.
- **Bandit territory**

  Meaning: An area or an industry, profession, etc., where rules and laws are ignored or flouted is bandit territory.
- **Bar fly**

  Meaning: A bar fly is a person who spends a lot of time drinking in different bars and pubs.
- **Barefaced liar**

  Meaning: A barefaced liar is one who displays no shame about lying even if they are exposed.
- **Bark is worse than their bite**

  Meaning: Someone who's bark is worse than their bite may well get angry and shout, but doesn't take action.
- **Barking up the wrong tree**

  Meaning: If you are barking up the wrong tree, it means that you have completely misunderstood something or are totally wrong.
- **Barkus is willing**

  Meaning: This idiom means that someone is willing to get married.

- **Barrack-room lawyer**

  Meaning: A barrack-room lawyer is a person who gives opinions on things they are not qualified to speak about.
- **Barrel of laughs**

  Meaning: If someone's a barrel of laughs, they are always joking and you find them funny.
- **Basket case**

  Meaning: If something is a basket case, it is so bad that it cannot be helped.
- **Bated breath**

  Meaning: If someone says they're waiting with bated breath, they're very excited and find it difficult to be patient.
- **Bats in the belfry**

  Meaning: Someone with bats in the belfry is crazy or eccentric.
- **Batten down the hatches**

  Meaning: If you batten down the hatches, you prepare for the worst that could happen to you.
- **Batting a thousand**

  Meaning: It means to do something perfectly.
- **Be all ears**

  Meaning: If you are all ears, you are very eager to hear what someone has to say.
- **Be on the pig's back**

  Meaning: If you're on the pig's back, you're happy / content / in fine form.
- **Be true blue**

  Meaning: If a person/object/situation is considered to be 'true blue', it is considered genuine.
- **Be up the spout**

  Meaning: If a woman is up the spout, she is pregnant.
- **Bean counter**

  Meaning: A bean counter is an accountant.

- **Bear fruit**

  Meaning: If something bears fruit, it produces positive results.
- **Bear market**

  Meaning: A bear market is a period when investors are pessimistic and expect financial losses so are more likely to sell than to buy shares.
- **Bear the brunt**

  Meaning: People who bear the brunt of something endure the worst of something bad.
- **Beard the lion in his own den**

  Meaning: If you confront a powerful or dangerous rival on their territory, you are bearding the lion in his own den.
- **Beat about the bush**

  Meaning: If someone doesn't say clearly what they mean and try to make it hard to understand, they are beating about the bush.
- **Beat someone to the draw**

  Meaning: If you beat someone to the draw, you do something before they do.
- **Beat swords into ploughshares**

  Meaning: If people beat swords into ploughshares, they spend money on humanitarian purposes rather than weapons.
- **Beat the rap**

  Meaning: If you beat the rap, you escape conviction and punishment for a crime or something you have done wrong.
- **Beat the tar out of**

  Meaning: When you want to beat the tar out of someone, you want to beat them up badly.
- **Beat to the punch**

  Meaning: If you beat someone to the punch, you act before them and gain an advantage.
- **Beat your brains out**

  Meaning: If you beat your brains out, you think hard about something but cannot solve, understand or remember it.

- **Beauty is in the eye of the beholder**

  Meaning: Beauty is in the eye of the beholder means that different people will find different things beautiful and that the differences of opinion don't matter greatly.
- **Beauty is only skin deep**

  Meaning: This idiom means that appearances can be deceptive and something that seems or looks good may turn out to be bad.
- **Beck and call**

  Meaning: Someone who does everything for you, no matter when you ask, is at your beck and call.
- **Bedroom eyes**

  Meaning: Someone with bedroom eyes has a sexy look in their eyes.
- **Bee in your bonnet**

  Meaning: If someone is very excited about something, they have a bee in their bonnet.
- **Bee's Knees**

  Meaning: If something is the bee's knees, it's outstanding or the best in its class.
- **Beeline for**

  Meaning: If you make a beeline for a place, you head there directly.
- **Been in the wars**

  Meaning: If someone has been in the wars, they have been hurt or look as if they have been in a struggle.
- **Been there, done that**

  Meaning: People say this when they have already experienced what is being discussed.
- **Beer and skittles**

  Meaning: People say that life is not all beer and skittles, meaning that it is not about self-indulgence and pleasure.
- **Before the ink is dry**

  Meaning: If people make an agreement or contract and then the situation changes very quickly, it changes before the ink is dry.

- **Beggars can't be choosers**

  Meaning: This idiom means that people who are in great need must accept any help that is offered, even if it is not a complete solution to their problems.

- **Behind bars**

  Meaning: When someone is behind bars, they are in prison.

- **Behind closed doors**

  Meaning: If something happens away from the public eye, it happens behind closed doors.

- **Behind someone's back**

  Meaning: If you do something behind someone's back, you do it without telling them.

- **Behind the curve**

  Meaning: If you are behind the curve, you are behind or out of touch with current trends or developments.

- **Behind the eight ball**

  Meaning: A difficult position from which it is unlikely one can escape.

- **Behind the times**

  Meaning: Someone that is behind the times is old-fashioned and has ideas that are regarded as out-dated.

- **Believe you me**

  Meaning: This is an emphatic way of saying 'believe me'.

- **Bell the cat**

  Meaning: To bell the cat is to perform a difficult or impossible task.

- **Bells and whistles**

  Meaning: Bells and whistles are attractive features that things like computer programmes have, though often a bit unnecessary.

- **Bells on**

  Meaning: To be somewhere with bells on means to arrive there happy and delighted to attend.

- **Belly up**

  Meaning: If things go belly up, they go badly wrong.
- **Below par**

  Meaning: If something isn't up to standard, or someone isn't feeling or doing very well, they are below par.
- **Below the belt**

  Meaning: If someone says something that is cruel or unfair, it is below the belt, like the illegal punches in boxing.
- **Belt and braces**

  Meaning: Someone who wears belt and braces is very cautious and takes no risks.
- **Bend over backwards**

  Meaning: If someone bends over backwards, they do everything they can to help someone.
- **Bend someone's ear**

  Meaning: To bend someone's ear is to talk to someone about something for a long-enough period that it becomes tiresome for the listener.
- **Beside the point**

  Meaning: If something is beside the point, it's not relevant to the matter being discussed or considered.
- **Beside themselves**

  Meaning: If people are beside themselves, they are very worried or emotional about something.
- **Best of both worlds**

  Meaning: If you have the best of both worlds, you benefit from different things that do not normally go together.
- **Best thing since sliced bread**

  Meaning: If something is the best thing since sliced bread, it is excellent.
- **Bet the farm**

  Meaning: If you bet the farm, you risk everything on something you think will succeed.

- **Bet the ranch**

  Meaning: If you bet the ranch, you risk everything on something you think will succeed.

- **Better late than never**

  Meaning: This idiom suggests that doing something late is better than not doing it at all.

- **Better safe than sorry**

  Meaning: This idiom is used to recommend being cautious rather than taking a risk.

- **Better than a kick in the teeth**

  Meaning: If something is better than a kick in the teeth, it isn't very good, but it is better than nothing.

- **Better than a stick in the eye**

  Meaning: If something is better than a stick in the eye, it isn't very good, but it is better than nothing.

- **Between the devil and the deep blue sea**

  Meaning: If you are caught between the devil and the deep blue sea, you are in a dilemma; a difficult choice.

- **Between you and me and the cat's whiskers**

  Meaning: This idiom is used when telling someone something that you want them to keep secret.

- **Beyond a shadow of a doubt**

  Meaning: If something's beyond a shadow of a doubt, then absolutely no doubts remain about it.

- **Beyond our ken**

  Meaning: If something's beyond your ken, it is beyond your understanding.

- **Beyond the black stump**

  Meaning: An Australian idiom indicating that even if you go as far as you can, the black stump is still a little further.

- **Beyond the pale**

  Meaning: If something's beyond the pale, it is too extreme to be acceptable morally or socially.

- **Big Apple**

  Meaning: The Big Apple is New York.
- **Big bucks**

  Meaning: If someone is making big bucks, they are making a lot of money.
- **Big cheese**

  Meaning: The big cheese is the boss.
- **Big fish**

  Meaning: An important person in a company or an organization is a big fish.
- **Big fish in a small pond**

  Meaning: A big fish in a small pond is an important person in a small place or organization.
- **Big hitter**

  Meaning: A big hitter is someone who commands a lot of respect and is very important in their field.
- **Big nose**

  Meaning: If someone has a big nose, it means they are excessively interested in everyone else's business.
- **Big picture**

  Meaning: The big picture of something is the overall perspective or objective, not the fine detail.
- **Big time**

  Meaning: This can be used to with the meaning 'very much'– if you like something big time, you like it a lot.
- **Bird's eye view**

  Meaning: If you have a bird's eye view of something, you can see it perfectly clearly.
- **Bird-brain**

  Meaning: Someone who has a bird-brain, or is bird-brained, is stupid.
- **Birds and the bees**

  Meaning: If a child is taught about the birds and the bees, they are taught about sex.

- **Birds of a feather flock together**

  Meaning: This idiom means that people with similar interests will stick together.
- **Birthday suit**

  Meaning: If you are in your birthday suit, you are naked.
- **Bit part**

  Meaning: A small part.
- **Bit player**

  Meaning: A bit player has a small or unimportant role in something.
- **Bite someone's head off**

  Meaning: If you bite someone's head off, you criticise them angrily.
- **Bite the bullet**

  Meaning: If you have to bite the bullet, you have to accept or face something unpleasant because it cannot be avoided.
- **Bite the dust**

  Meaning: This is a way of saying that somebody has died, especially if they are killed violently like a soldier in battle.
- **Bite your lip**

  Meaning: If you have to bite your lip, you have to make a conscious effort not to react or to keep quiet about something that displeases you.
- **Bite your tongue**

  Meaning: If you bite your tongue, you refrain from speaking because it is socially or otherwise better not to.
- **Bits and bobs**

  Meaning: Bits and bobs are small, remnant articles and things-the same as 'odds and ends'.
- **Bitter end**

  Meaning: If you do something to the bitter end, you do it to the very end, no matter how unsuccessful you are.
- **Bitter pill to swallow**

  Meaning: A bitter pill to swallow is something that is hard to accept.

- **Black and blue**

  Meaning: This means bruised, either physically or metaphorically.

- **Black and white**

  Meaning: When it is very clear who or what is right and wrong, then the situation is black and white.

- **Black hole**

  Meaning: If there is a black hole in financial accounts, money has disappeared.

- **Black sheep**

  Meaning: Someone who is the black sheep doesn't fit into a group or family because their behaviour or character is not good enough.

- **Blank slate**

  Meaning: A blank slate is something that hasn't been developed or described in any detail.

- **Bleeding heart**

  Meaning: A bleeding heart is a person who is excessively sympathetic towards other people.

- **Blessing in disguise**

  Meaning: If some bad luck or misfortune ultimately results in something positive, it's a blessing in disguise.

- **Blind acceptance**

  Meaning: If people accept thing blindly, they accept them without questioning them at all.

- **Blink of an eye**

  Meaning: If something happens in the blink of an eye, it happens so fast it is almost impossible to notice it.

- **Blood is thicker than water**

  Meaning: This idiom means that family relationships are stronger than others.

- **Blood out of a stone**

  Meaning: If something is like getting blood out of a stone, it is very difficult indeed.

- **Blood, sweat and tears**

  Meaning: If something will take blood, sweat and tears, it will be very difficult and will require a lot of effort and sacrifice.
- **Blow a fuse**

  Meaning: If you blow a fuse, you become uncontrollably angry.
- **Blow by blow**

  Meaning: A blow-by-blow description gives every detail in sequence.
- **Blow hot and cold**

  Meaning: If you blow hot and cold on an idea, your attitude and opinion keeps changing; one minute you are for it, the next you are against.
- **Blow out of the water**

  Meaning: If something, like an idea, is blown out of the water, it is destroyed or defeated comprehensively.
- **Blow smoke**

  Meaning: If people blow smoke, they exaggerate or say things that are not true, usually to make themselves look better.
- **Blow the cobwebs away**

  Meaning: If you blow the cobwebs away, you make sweeping changes to something to bring fresh views and ideas in.
- **Blow the whistle**

  Meaning: If somebody blows the whistle on a plan, they report it to the authorities.
- **Blow your mind**

  Meaning: Something that will blow your mind is something extraordinary that will amaze you beyond explanation.
- **Blow your own horn**

  Meaning: If you blow your own horn, you boast about your achievements and abilities.
- **Blow your own trumpet**

  Meaning: If someone blows their own trumpet, they boast about their talents and achievements.

- **Blow your stack**
  Meaning: If you blow your stack, you lose your temper.
- **Blow your top**
  Meaning: If someone blows their top, they lose their temper.

C

- **Cake's not worth the candle**
  Meaning: If someone says that the cake's not worth the candle, they mean that the result will not be worth the effort put in to achieve it.
- **Calf lick**
  Meaning: A calf lick is the weird parting in your fringe where your hair grows in a different direction, usually to one side.
- **Call a spade a spade**
  Meaning: A person who calls a spade a spade is one speaks frankly and makes little or no attempt to conceal their opinions or to spare the feelings of their audience.
- **Call it a day**
  Meaning: If you call it a day, you stop doing something for a while, normally at least until the following day.
- **Call on the carpet**
  Meaning: If you are called on the carpet, you are summoned for a reprimand by superiors or others in power.
- **Call the dogs off**
  Meaning: If someone calls off their dogs, they stop attacking or criticising someone.
- **Call the shots**
  Meaning: If you call the shots, you are in charge and tell people what to do.
- **Call the tune**
  Meaning: The person who calls the tune makes the important decisions about something.
- **Calm before the storm**
  Meaning: A calm time immediately before period of violent activity or argument is the calm before the storm.

- **Can of worms**

  Meaning: If an action can create serious problems, it is opening a can of worms.
- **Can't dance and it's too wet to plow**

  Meaning: When you can't dance and it's too wet to plow, you may as well do something because you can't or don't have the opportunity to do anything else.
- **Can't do it for toffee**

  Meaning: If you can't so something for toffee, you are incapable of doing something properly or to any sort of standard.
- **Can't get a word in edgeways**

  Meaning: If you can't get a word in edgeways, you don't have the chance to say anything because the person you are with is talking all the time.
- **Can't get to 1st base**

  Meaning: If you can't get to first base, you're having difficulties starting something.
- **Can't hack it**

  Meaning: Unable to perform an act, duty, job etc.
- **Can't hold a candle**

  Meaning: If something can't hold a candle to something else, it is much worse.
- **Can't see the forest for its trees**

  Meaning: If someone can't see the forest for its trees, they are too focused on specific details to see the picture as a whole.
- **Canary in a coal mine**

  Meaning: A canary in a coal mine is an early warning of danger.
- **Card up your sleeve**

  Meaning: If you have a card up your sleeve, you have a surprise plan or idea that you are keeping back until the time is right.
- **Carpet bagger**

  Meaning: A carpetbagger is an opportunist without any scruples or ethics, or a politician who wants to represent a place they have no connection with.

- **Carrot and stick**

  Meaning: If someone offers a carrot and stick, they offer an incentive to do something combined with the threat of punishment.

- **Carry the day**

  Meaning: If something carries the day, it wins a battle or competition for supremacy.

- **Case by case**

  Meaning: If things are done case by case, each situation or issue is handled separately on its own merits and demerits.

- **Cash cow**

  Meaning: A product, business, etc., that generates a continuous flow of money or a high proportion of overall profits is a cash cow.

- **Cash in your chips**

  Meaning: If you cash in your chips, you sell something to get what profit you can because you think its value is going to fall. It can also mean 'to die'.

- **Cast a long shadow**

  Meaning: Something or someone that casts a long shadow has considerable influence on other people or events.

- **Cast aspersion**

  Meaning: If you cast aspersion, you try to blacken someone's name and make people think badly of them.

- **Cast doubt on**

  Meaning: If you make other people not sure about a matter, then you have cast doubt on it.

- **Cast iron stomach**

  Meaning: A person with a cast iron stomach can eat or drink anything without any ill effects.

- **Cast pearls before swine**

  Meaning: If you cast pearls before swine, you offer

something of value to someone who doesn't appreciate it- 'swine' are 'pigs'.

- **Cast sheep's eyes at**

  Meaning: If you cast sheep's eyes at someone, you look lovingly or with longing at them.
- **Cast your net widely**

  Meaning: If you cast your net widely, you use a wide range of sources when trying to find something.
- **Casting vote**

  Meaning: The casting vote is a vote given to a chairman or president that is used when there is a deadlock.
- **Castles in the air**

  Meaning: Plans that are impractical and will never work out are castles in the air.
- **Cat among the pigeons**

  Meaning: If something or someone puts, or sets or lets, the cat among the pigeons, they create a disturbance and cause trouble.
- **Cat and dog life**

  Meaning: If people lead a cat and dog life, they are always arguing.
- **Cat burglar**

  Meaning: A cat burglar is a skilful thief who breaks into places without disturbing people or setting off alarms.
- **Cat got your tongue?**

  Meaning: If someone asks if the cat has got your tongue, they want to know why you are not speaking when they think you should.
- **Cat nap**

  Meaning: If you have a short sleep during the day, you are cat napping.
- **Cat's lick**

  Meaning: A cat's lick is a very quick wash.
- **Cat's pajamas**

  Meaning: Something that is the cat's pajamas is excellent.

- **Cat went to pray after eating 900 rats**
  Meaning: Pretending to be innocent after many sins.
- **Cat's whiskers**
  Meaning: Something excellent is the cat's whiskers.
- **Catch as catch can**
  Meaning: This means that people should try to get something any way they can.
- **Catch hell**
  Meaning: If you catch hell, you get into trouble or get scolded.
- **Catch some z's**
  Meaning: If you catch some z's, you get some sleep.
- **Catch someone red-handed**
  Meaning: If someone is caught red-handed, they are found doing something wrong or illegal.
- **Caught with your hand in the cookie jar**
  Meaning: If someone is caught with his or her hand in the cookie jar, he or she is caught doing something wrong.
- **Chalk and cheese**
  Meaning: Things, or people, that are like chalk and cheese are very different and have nothing in common.
- **Champ at the bit**
  Meaning: If someone is champing at the bit, they are very eager to accomplish something.
- **Champagne taste on a beer budget**
  Meaning: Someone who lives above their means and likes things they cannot afford has champagne taste on a beer budget.
- **Change of heart**
  Meaning: If you change the way you think or feel about something, you have a change of heart.
- **Change tack**
  Meaning: If you change tack, you use a different method for dealing with something.
- **Change your tune**
  Meaning: If someone changes their ideas or the way they talk about them, they change their tune.

- **Chapter and verse**

  Meaning: When you know something very well, and can quote it, you know it chapter and verse.
- **Charity begins at home**

  Meaning: This idiom means that family members are more important than anyone else, and should be the focus of a person's efforts.
- **Chase rainbows**

  Meaning: If someone chases rainbows, they try to do something that they will never achieve.
- **Chase your tail**

  Meaning: If you are chasing your tail, you are very busy but not being very productive.
- **Cheap as chips**

  Meaning: If something is very inexpensive, it is as cheap as chips.
- **Cheap at half the price**

  Meaning: If something's cheap at half the price, it's very cheap indeed.
- **Cheap shot**

  Meaning: A cheap shot is an unprincipled criticism.
- **Cheat death**

  Meaning: If someone cheats death, they narrowly avoid a major problem or accident.
- **Cheek by jowl**

  Meaning: If things or people are cheek by jowl, they are very close together.
- **Cherry pick**

  Meaning: If people cherry pick, they choose things that support their position, while ignoring things that contradict it.
- **Chew on a bone**

  Meaning: If someone is chewing on a bone, he or she is thinking about something intently.

- **Chew the cud**

  Meaning: If you chew the cud, you think carefully about something.

- **Chew the fat**

  Meaning: If you chew the fat with someone, you talk at leisure with them.

- **Chicken feed**

  Meaning: If something is small or unimportant, especially money, it is chickenfeed.

- **Child's play**

  Meaning: If something is child's play, it is very easy and simple.

- **Chip off the old block**

  Meaning: If someone is a chip off the old block, they closely resemble one or both of the parents in character.

- **Chip on your shoulder**

  Meaning: If someone has a chip on their shoulder, they are resentful about something and feel that they have been treated badly.

- **Chomping at the bit**

  Meaning: If you are chomping at the bit, you are eager to start on a task immediately.

- **Chop and change**

  Meaning: If things chop and change, they keep changing, often unexpectedly.

- **Cigarette paper**

  Meaning: If you cannot get or put a cigarette paper between people, they are so closely bonded that nothing will separate them or their positions on issues.

- **Circle the drain**

  Meaning: If someone is circling the drain, they are spiraling downward to a usually inevitable death.

- **Class act**

  Meaning: Someone who's a class act is exceptional in what they do.

- **Clean bill of health**

  Meaning: If something or someone has a clean bill of health, then there's nothing wrong; everything's fine.
- **Clean break**

  Meaning: If you make a clean break, you break away completely from something.
- **Clean hands**

  Meaning: Someone with clean hands, or who keeps their hands clean, is not involved in illegal or immoral activities.
- **Clean slate**

  Meaning: If you start something with a clean slate, then nothing bad from your past is taken into account.
- **Clean sweep**

  Meaning: If someone makes a clean sweep, they win absolutely everything in a competition or contest.
- **Clean your clock**

  Meaning: If you clean your clock, you beat someone decisively in a contest or fight.
- **Clear as a bell**

  Meaning: If something is as clear as a bell, it is very clear or easy to understand.
- **Clear as mud**

  Meaning: If something is as clear as mud, then it is very confusing and unclear.
- **Clear the decks**

  Meaning: When you clear the decks, you get ready for an important action and put away items that might get in your way.
- **Climb on the bandwagon**

  Meaning: When people climb on the bandwagon they do something because it is popular and everyone else is doing it.
- **Climb the greasy pole**

  Meaning: Advance within an organization – especially in politics.

- **Cling to hope**

  Meaning: If people cling to hope, they continue to hope though the chances of success are very small.

- **Close at hand**

  Meaning: If something is close at hand, it is nearby or conveniently located.

- **Close but no cigar**

  Meaning: If you are close but no cigar, you are close to success or the truth, but have not got there.

- **Close lipped**

  Meaning: A person who is reluctant to talk about a specific subject is close lipped.

- **Close only counts in horseshoes and hand grenades**

  Meaning: This phrase is used to say that if you come close to success without succeeding, it is not good enough.

- **Close shave**

  Meaning: If you have a close shave, you very nearly have a serious accident or get into trouble.

- **Close the book**

  Meaning: If you close the book on something, you end it completely.

- **Close to your heart**

  Meaning: If something is close to your heart, you care a lot about it.

- **Closed book to me**

  Meaning: If a subject is a closed book to you, it is something that you don't understand or know anything about.

- **Cloth ears**

  Meaning: If you don't listen to people, they may suggest you have cloth ears.

- **Cloud cuckoo land**

  Meaning: If someone has ideas or plans that are completely unrealistic, they are living on cloud cuckoo land.

- **Cloud of suspicion**
  Meaning: If a cloud of suspicion hangs over an individual, it means that they are not believed or are distrusted.
- **Cloud on the horizon**
  Meaning: If you can see a problem ahead, you can call it a cloud on the horizon.
- **Coals to Newcastle**
  Meaning: Taking, bringing, or carrying coals to Newcastle is doing something that is completely unnecessary.
- **Coast is clear**
  Meaning: When the coast is clear, the people supposed to be watching you are not there and you are able to move or leave.
- **Cock a snook**
  Meaning: To make a rude gesture by putting one thumb to the nose with the fingers outstretched.
- **Cock and bull story**
  Meaning: A cock and bull story is a lie someone tells that is completely unbelievable.
- **Cock in the henhouse**
  Meaning: This is used to describe a male in an all-female environment.
- **Cock of the walk**
  Meaning: A man who is excessively confident and thinks he's better than other people is the cock of the walk.
- **Cog in the machine**
  Meaning: A person who does an unimportant job in a large company or organization is a cog in the machine.
- **Cold feet**
  Meaning: If you get cold feet about something, you lose the courage to do it.
- **Cold fish**
  Meaning: A cold fish is a person who doesn't show how they feel.

- **Cold light of day**

  Meaning: If you see things in the cold light of day, you see them as they really are, not as you might want them to be.
- **Cold shoulder**

  Meaning: If you give or show someone the cold shoulder, you are deliberately unfriendly and uncooperative towards them.
- **Cold sweat**

  Meaning: If something brings you out in a cold sweat, it frightens you a lot.
- **Cold turkey**

  Meaning: If someone suddenly stops taking drugs, instead of slowly cutting down, they do cold turkey.
- **Colder than a witch's tit**

  Meaning: If it is colder than a witch's tit, it is extremely cold outside.
- **Collateral damage**

  Meaning: Accidental or unintended damage or casualties are collateral damage.
- **Collect dust**

  Meaning: If something is collecting dust, it isn't being used anymore.
- **Colour bar**

  Meaning: Rules that restrict access on the basis of race or ethnicity are a colour bar.
- **Come a cropper**

  Meaning: Someone whose actions or lifestyle will inevitably result in trouble is going to come a cropper.
- **Come clean**

  Meaning: If someone comes clean about something, they admit to deceit or wrongdoing.
- **Come hell or high water**

  Meaning: If someone says they'll do something come hell or high water, they mean that nothing will stop them, no matter what happens.

- **Come on hard**

  Meaning: If you come on hard, you are aggressive in your dealing with someone.
- **Come on the heels of**

  Meaning: If something comes on the heels of something, it follows very soon after it.
- **Come out in the wash**

  Meaning: If something will come out in the wash, it won't have any permanent negative effect.
- **Come out of the woodwork**

  Meaning: When things come out of the woodwork, they appear unexpectedly.
- **Come out of your shell**

  Meaning: If someone comes out of their shell, they stop being shy and withdrawn and become more friendly and sociable.
- **Come to a head**

  Meaning: If events reach a crisis point, they come to a head.
- **Come to a pretty pass**

  Meaning: If something has come to a pretty pass, then it is in a difficult, unfavourable or negative situation.
- **Come to bear**

  Meaning: If something comes to bear on you, you start to feel the pressure or effect of it.
- **Come to call**

  Meaning: If someone comes to call, they respond to an order or summons directly.
- **Come to grips**

  Meaning: If you come to grips with a problem or issue, you face up to it and deal with it.
- **Come up smelling of roses**

  Meaning: If someone comes up smelling of roses, they emerge from a situation with their reputation undamaged.
- **Come what may**

  Meaning: If you're prepared to do something come what may, it means that nothing will stop or distract you, no matter how hard or difficult it becomes.

- **Come with the territory**

  Meaning: If something comes with the territory, it is part of a job or responsibility and just has to be accepted, even if unpleasant.

- **Confirmed bachelor**

  Meaning: A confirmed bachelor is a man who shows little or no interest in women. It can be used to suggest that they're gay.

- **Connect the dots**

  Meaning: When you connect the dots, you understand the connections and relationships.

- **Constitution of an ox**

  Meaning: If someone has the constitution of an ox, they are less affected than most people by things like tiredness, illness, alcohol, etc.

- **Cook someone's goose**

  Meaning: If you cook someone's goose, you ruin their plans.

- **Cook the books**

  Meaning: If people cook the books, they keep false accounts to make money illegally or avoid paying tax.

- **Cooking with gas**

  Meaning: If you're cooking with gas, you're working very efficiently.

- **Cool as a cat**

  Meaning: To act fine when you a actually scared or nervous.

- **Cool your heels**

  Meaning: If you leave someone to cool their heels, you make them wait until they have calmed down.

- **Coon's age**

  Meaning: A very long time, as in 'I haven't seen her in a coon's age!'

- **Corner a market**

  Meaning: If a business is dominant in an area and unlikely to be challenged by other companies, it has cornered the market.

- **Couch potato**

  Meaning: A couch potato is an extremely idle or lazy person who chooses to spend most of their leisure time horizontal in front of the TV and eats a diet that is mainly junk food.

- **Could eat a horse**

  Meaning: If you are very hungry, you could eat a horse.

- **Couldn't give two hoots**

  Meaning: If you couldn't give two hoots about something, you don't care at all about it.

- **Count sheep**

  Meaning: If people cannot sleep, they are advised to count sheep mentally.

- **Count your blessings**

  Meaning: When people count their blessings, they concentrate on all the good things in their lives instead of the negative ones.

- **Country mile**

  Meaning: A country mile is used to describe a long distance.

- **Cover all the bases**

  Meaning: If you cover all the bases, you deal with all aspects of a situation or issue, or anticipate all possibilities.

- **Crack a nut with a sledgehammer**

  Meaning: If you use a sledgehammer to crack a nut, you apply too much force to achieve a result.

- **Crack of dawn**

  Meaning: The crack of dawn is very early in the morning.

- **Crash a party**

  Meaning: If you crash a party, or are a gatecrasher, you go somewhere you haven't been invited to.

- **Cream of the crop**

  Meaning: The cream of the crop is the best there is.

- **Cream rises to the top**

  Meaning: A good person or idea cannot go unnoticed for long, just as cream poured in coffee or tea eventually rises to the top.

- **Crepe hanger**

  Meaning: One who always looks at the bad side of things and is morbid or gloomy. In olden days crepe was hung on the door of a deceased person's home.

- **Crocodile tears**

  Meaning: If someone cries crocodile tears, they pretend to be upset or affected by something.

- **Crooked as a dog's hind leg**

  Meaning: Someone who is very dishonest is as crooked as a dog's hind leg.

- **Cross my heart and hope to die**

  Meaning: People say this to show how sincere their promise is.

- **Cross that bridge when you come to it**

  Meaning: If you will cross that bridge when you come to it, you will deal with a problem when it arises, but not until that point.

- **Cross to bear**

  Meaning: If someone has a cross to bear, they have a heavy burden of responsibility or a problem that they alone must cope with.

- **Crunch time**

  Meaning: When people, companies, etc., have to make an important decision that will have a considerable effect on their future, it is crunch time.

- **Cry wolf**

  Meaning: If someone cries wolf, they raise a false alarm about something.

- **Cry your eyes out**

  Meaning: If you cry your eyes out, you cry uncontrollably.

- **Cry-baby**

  Meaning: A cry-baby is a person who gets emotional and cries too easily.

- **Cuckoo in the nest**

  Meaning: Is an issue or a problem, etc., is a cuckoo in the nest, it grows quickly and crowds out.
- **Cumin in camel's mouth**

  Meaning: A very small gain as compared to the larger gain expected.
- **Cupboard love**

  Meaning: To show love to gain something from someone.
- **Curate's egg**

  Meaning: If something is a bit of a curate's egg, it is only good in parts.
- **Curdle your blood**

  Meaning: If something is very frightening or disturbing, it curdles your blood.

D

- **Daft as a brush**

  Meaning: Someone who is daft as a brush is rather stupid.
- **Damp squib**

  Meaning: If something is expected to have a great effect or impact but doesn't, it is a damp squib.
- **Dancing on someone's grave**

  Meaning: If you will dance on someone's grave, you will outlive or outlast them and will celebrate their demise.
- **Dark horse**

  Meaning: If someone is a dark horse, they are a bit of a mystery and we don't know how they will react or perform.
- **Daylight robbery**

  Meaning: If you are overcharged or underpaid, it is a daylight robbery; open, unfair and hard to prevent. Rip-off has a similar meaning.
- **Days are numbered**

  Meaning: When someone's days are numbered, they are expected to die soon.

- **Dead air**

  Meaning: When there is a period of total silence, there is dead air.

- **Dead and buried**

  Meaning: If something is dead and buried, it has all long been settled and is not going to be.

- **Dead as a dodo**

  Meaning: If something's dead as a dodo, it is lifeless and dull.

- **Dead as a doornail**

  Meaning: This is used to indicate that something is lifeless.

- **Dead duck**

  Meaning: If something is a dead duck, it is a failure.

- **Dead even**

  Meaning: If people competing are dead even, they are at exactly the same stage or moving at exactly the same speed.

- **Dead from the neck up**

  Meaning: Someone who's dead from the neck up is very stupid indeed.

- **Dead heat**

  Meaning: If a race ends in a dead heat, two or more finish with exactly the same result.

- **Dead in the water**

  Meaning: If something is dead in the water, it isn't going anywhere or making any progress.

- **Dead level best**

  Meaning: If you try your dead level best, you try as hard as you possibly could to do something.

- **Dead meat**

  Meaning: This is used as a way of threatening someone: You'll be dead meat if you don't go along.

- **Dead men's shoes**

  Meaning: If promotion or success requires replacing somebody, then it can only be reached by dead men's shoes' by getting rid of them.

- **Dead right**

  Meaning: This means that something or someone is absolutely correct, without doubt.

- **Dead to the world**

  Meaning: If somebody's fast asleep and completely unaware of what is happening around them, he or she's dead to the world.

- **Dead wrong**

  Meaning: If someone is dead wrong, they are absolutely in error, absolutely incorrect or of incorrect opinion.

- **Deaf as a post**

  Meaning: Someone who is as deaf as a post is unable to hear at all.

- **Death warmed up**

  Meaning: If someone looks like death warmed up, they look very ill indeed.

- **Decorate the mahogany**

  Meaning: When someone buys a round a pub or bar, they decorate the mahogany; putting cash on the bar.

- **Deep pockets**

  Meaning: If someone has deep pockets, they are wealthy.

- **Deep pockets but short arms**

  Meaning: Someone who has money but never puts his hand in his pocket to pay for anything has deep pockets but short arms.

- **Deer in the headlights**

  Meaning: When one is caught offguard and needs to make a decision, but cannot react quickly.

- **Deliver the goods**

  Meaning: Do what is required, come up to expectations.

- **Demon weed**

  Meaning: Tobacco is the demon weed.

- **Derring-do**

  Meaning: If a person shows derring-do, they show great courage.

- **Devil may care**

  Meaning: If you live a devil-may-care life it means you are willing to take more risks than most people.
- **Devil's advocate**

  Meaning: If someone plays Devil's advocate in an argument, they adopt a position they don't believe in just for the sake of the argument
- **Diamond in the rough**

  Meaning: A diamond in the rough is someone or something that has great potential, but isn't not refined and polished.
- **Die is cast**

  Meaning: If the die is cast, a decision has been made that cannot be altered and fate will decide the consequences.
- **Different kettle of fish**

  Meaning: If something is a different kettle of fish, it is very different from the other things referenced.
- **Different ropes for different folks**

  Meaning: This idiom means that different people do things in different ways that suit them.
- **Different strokes for different folks**

  Meaning: This idiom means that different people do things in different ways that suit them.
- **Dig way down deep**

  Meaning: When someone digs way down deep, they look into their inner feelings to see how they feel about it.
- **Dig your heels in**

  Meaning: If you dig your heels in, you start to resist something.
- **Dime a dozen**

  Meaning: If something is a dime a dozen, it is extremely common, possibly too common.
- **Dine on ashes**

  Meaning: I someone is dining on ashes he or she is excessively focusing attention on failures or regrets for past actions.

- **Dinosaur**

  Meaning: A dinosaur is a person who is thought to be too old for their position.
- **Dip your toes in the water**

  Meaning: If you dip your toes in the water, you try something tentatively because you are not sure whether it will work or not.
- **Dirty dog**

  Meaning: A dirty dog is an untrustworthy person.
- **Discerning eye**

  Meaning: If a person has a discerning eye, they are particularly good at judging the quality of something.
- **Discretion is the better part of valour**

  Meaning: This idiom means that it is often better to think carefully and not act than to do something that may cause problems.
- **Dish the dirt**

  Meaning: If you dish the dirt on something or someone, you make unpleasant or shocking information public.
- **Do a runner**

  Meaning: If people leave a restaurant without paying, they do a runner.
- **Do as you would be done by**

  Meaning: Treat and respect others as you would hope to be respected and treated by them.
- **Do the needful**

  Meaning: If you do the needful, you do what is necessary.
- **Do the running**

  Meaning: The person who has to do the running has to make sure that things get done.
- **Do time**

  Meaning: When someone is doing time, they are in prison.
- **Do's and don't's**

  Meaning: The do's and don't's are what is acceptable or allowed or not within an area or issue, etc.

- **Dodge the bullet**

  Meaning: If someone has dodged a bullet, they have successfully avoided a very serious problem.
- **Dog and pony show**

  Meaning: A dog and pony show is a presentation or some marketing that has lots of style, but no real content.
- **Dog days**

  Meaning: Dog days are very hot summer days.
- **Dog eat dog**

  Meaning: In a dog eat dog world, there is intense competition and rivalry, where everybody thinks only of himself or herself.
- **Dog in the manger**

  Meaning: If someone acts like a dog in the manger, they don't want other people to have or enjoy things that are useless to them.
- **Dog tired**

  Meaning: If you are dog tired, you are exhausted.
- **Dog's dinner**

  Meaning: Something that is a dog's dinner is a real mess.
- **Dog's life**

  Meaning: If some has a dog's life, they have a very unfortunate and wretched life.
- **Dog-eared**

  Meaning: If a book is dog-eared, it is in bad condition, with torn pages, etc.
- **Dog-whistle politics**

  Meaning: When political parties have policies that will appeal to racists while not being overtly racist, they are indulging in dog-whistle politics.
- **Doggy bag**

  Meaning: If you ask for a doggy bag in a restaurant, they will pack the food you haven't eaten for you to take home.
- **Doldrums**

  Meaning: If a person is in the doldrums, they are depressed. If a project or something similar is in the doldrums, it isn't making any progress.

- **Dollars for doughnuts**

  Meaning: If something is dollars for doughnuts, it is a sure bet or certainty.

- **Don't bite the hand that feeds**

  Meaning: When someone says this to you, they are trying to tell you not to act against those on whom you depend.

- **Don't cry over spilt milk**

  Meaning: When something bad happens and nothing can be done to help it people say, 'Don't cry over spilt milk'.

- **Don't give up the day job**

  Meaning: This idiom is used a way of telling something that they do something badly.

- **Don't hold your breath**

  Meaning: If you are told not to hold your breath, it means that you shouldn't have high expectations about something.

- **Don't look a gift horse in the mouth**

  Meaning: This means that if you are given something, a present or a chance, you should not waste it by being too critical or examining it too closely.

- **Don't mention the war**

  Meaning: This means that you shouldn't speak about things that could cause an argument or tension.

- **Don't push my buttons!**

  Meaning: This can be said to someone who is starting to annoy you.

- **Don't shoot the messenger**

  Meaning: This phrase can be used when breaking some bad news to someone and you don't want to be blamed for the news.

- **Don't stand there with curlers in your hair**

  Meaning: This means 'don't keep me waiting'. It's said to someone who is taking too long to get moving.

- **Don't sweat the small stuff**

  Meaning: This is used to tell people not to worry about trivial or unimportant issues.

- **Don't take any wooden nickels**

  Meaning: This idiom is used to advise people not to be cheated or ripped off.

- **Don't throw bricks when you live in a glass house**

  Meaning: Don't call others out on actions that you, yourself do. Don't be a hypocrite.

- **Don't upset the applecart**

  Meaning: If you are advised not to upset the applecart, you are being told not to disturb the way things are done because it might ruin things.

- **Done to death**

  Meaning: If a joke or story has been done to death, it has been told so often that it has stopped being funny.

- **Donkey work**

  Meaning: Donkey work is any hard, boring work or task.

- **Donkey's years**

  Meaning: This idiom means 'a very long time'.

- **Doormat**

  Meaning: A person who doesn't stand up for themselves and gets treated badly is a doormat.

- **Double Dutch**

  Meaning: If something is double Dutch, it is completely incomprehensible.

- **Double take**

  Meaning: If someone does a double take, they react very slowly to something to show how shocked or surprised they are.

- **Double whammy**

  Meaning: A double whammy is when something causes two problems at the same time, or when two setbacks occur at the same time.

- **Double-edged sword**

  Meaning: If someone uses an argument that could both help them and harm them, then they are using a double-edged sword; it cuts both ways.

- **Doubting Thomas**

  Meaning: A Doubting Thomas is someone who only believes what they see themselves, not what they are told.

- **Down and dirty**

  Meaning: Down and dirty means unscrupulous and very competitive.

- **Down and out**

  Meaning: If someone is down and out, they are desperately poor and need help.

- **Down at heel**

  Meaning: Someone who is down at heel is short of money.

- **Down for the count**

  Meaning: If someone is down for the count, they have lost a struggle, like a boxer who has been knocked out.

- **Down in the doldrums**

  Meaning: If somebody's down in the doldrums, they are depressed and lacking energy.

- **Down in the mouth**

  Meaning: If someone is down in the mouth, they look unhappy or depressed.

- **Down the drain**

  Meaning: If something goes down the drain, especially money or work, it is wasted or produces no results.

- **Down the hatch**

  Meaning: This idiom can be said before drinking alcohol in company.

- **Down the pan**

  Meaning: If something has gone down the pan, it has failed or been ruined.

- **Down the pike**

  Meaning: Something that is down the pike it is in the future.
- **Down the tubes**

  Meaning: If something has gone down the tubes, it has failed or been ruined.
- **Down to the wire**

  Meaning: If something goes down to the wire, like a competition, then it goes to the very last moment before it is clear who has won.
- **Down-to-earth**

  Meaning: Someone who's down-to-earth is practical and realistic. It can also be used for things like ideas.
- **Drag your feet**

  Meaning: If someone is dragging their feet, they are taking too long to do or finish something, usually because they don't want to do it.
- **Drag your heels**

  Meaning: If you drag your heels, you either delay doing something or do it as slowly as possible because you don't want to do it.
- **Draw a bead on**

  Meaning: To draw a bead on is to aim a gun at something and can be used to mean to focus on or aim at something as a goal.
- **Draw a blank**

  Meaning: If you try to find something out and draw a blank, you don't get any useful information.
- **Draw a line in the sand**

  Meaning: If you draw a line in the sand, you establish a limit beyond which things will be unacceptable.
- **Draw a long bow**

  Meaning: If someone draws a long bow, they lie or exaggerate.
- **Draw the line**

  Meaning: When you draw the line, you set out limits of what you find acceptable, beyond which you will not go.

- **Draw the shortest straw**

  Meaning: If someone draws the shortest straw, they lose or are chosen to do something unpleasant.

- **Drawing card**

  Meaning: A famous person who attracts people to attend an event is a drawing card.

- **Dress someone down**

  Meaning: If you dress someone down, you scold them.

- **Dress to kill**

  Meaning: When someone is dressed to kill, they are dressed very smartly.

- **Dressed to the nines**

  Meaning: If you are in your very best clothes, you're dressed to the nines.

- **Drink like a fish**

  Meaning: If someone drinks like a fish, they drink far too much alcohol.

- **Drive a wedge**

  Meaning: If you drive a wedge between people, you exploit an issue so that people start to disagree.

- **Drive someone up the wall**

  Meaning: If something or someone drives you up the wall, they do something that irritates you greatly.

- **Drive you spare**

  Meaning: If someone or something drives you spare, it is extremely annoying.

- **Driven by a motor**

  Meaning: This is used to describe people with Attention Deficit Hyperactivity Disorder when they talk excessively: 'they act as if driven by a motor.'

- **Drop a bombshell**

  Meaning: If someone drops a bombshell, they announce something that changes a situation drastically and unexpectedly.

- **Drop a dime**

  Meaning: If you drop a dime, you inform the police about someone's illegal activities.

- **Drop in the bucket**

  Meaning: A drop in the bucket is something so small that it won't make any noticeable difference.

- **Drop in the ocean**

  Meaning: A drop in the ocean implies that something will have little effect because it is small and mostly insignificant.

- **Drop into your lap**

  Meaning: If something drops into your lap, you receive it suddenly, without any warning.

- **Drop someone a line**

  Meaning: If you drop someone a line, you send a letter to them.

- **Dropped like a hot cake**

  Meaning: If something is dropped like a hot cake, it is rejected or disposed of very quickly.

- **Drown your sorrows**

  Meaning: If someone gets drunk or drinks a lot to try to stop feeling unhappy, they drown their sorrows.

- **Drunk as a lord**

  Meaning: Someone who is very drunk is as drunk as a lord.

- **Drunker than a peach orchard boar**

  Meaning: Very drunk, as when a boar would eat fermented peaches that have fallen from the tree.

- **Dry as a bone**

  Meaning: If your lawn is as dry as a bone, the soil is completely dry.

- **Dry as a wooden god**

  Meaning: Very dry area or very thirsty: That desert is as dry as a wooden god.

- **Dry as snuff**

  Meaning: If something is as dry as snuff, it is very dry indeed.

- **Dry run**

  Meaning: A dry run is a full rehearsal or trial exercise of something to see how it will work before it is launched.
- **Dry spell**

  Meaning: If something or someone is having a dry spell, they aren't being as successful as they normally are.
- **Duck soup**

  Meaning: If something is duck soup, it is very easy.
- **Duck to water**

  Meaning: If you take to something like a duck to water, you find when you start that you have a natural affinity for it.
- **Ducks in a row**

  Meaning: If you have your ducks in a row, you are well-organized.
- **Dumb as a post**

  Meaning: Someone's who's as dumb as a post is very stupid, like a fencepost.
- **Dumb as a rock**

  Meaning: If you are dumb as a rock, you have no common sense and are stupid.
- **Dunkirk spirit**

  Meaning: Dunkirk spirit is when people pull together to get through a very difficult time.
- **Dutch courage**

  Meaning: Dutch courage is the reckless bravery caused by drinking too much.
- **Dutch treat**

  Meaning: If something like a meal is a Dutch treat, then each person pays their own share of the bill.
- **Dutch uncle**

  Meaning: A Dutch uncle is a person who gives unwelcome advice.
- **Dutch wife**

  Meaning: A Dutch wife is a long pillow or a hot water bottle.

- **Dwell on the past**

  Meaning: Thinking too much about the past, so that it becomes a problem is to dwell on the past.
- **Dyed-in-the-wool**

  Meaning: If someone is a dyed-in-the-wool supporter of a political party, etc., they support them totally, without any questions.

E

- **Eager beaver**

  Meaning: A person who is extremely keen is an eager beaver.
- **Eagle eyes**

  Meaning: Someone who has eagle eyes sees everything; no detail is too small.
- **Early bath**

  Meaning: If someone has or goes for an early bath, they quit or lose their job or position earlier than expected because things have gone wrong.
- **Early bird catches the worm**

  Meaning: The early bird catches the worm means that if you start something early, you stand a better chance of success.
- **Early to bed, early to rise, makes a man healthy wealthy and wise**

  Meaning: It means that sleeping well and not staying up late will help you out physically and financially.
- **Earn a living**

  Meaning: To make money.
- **Easy as beans**

  Meaning: Something that is so easy that anyone can do it is easy as beans.
- **Easy as falling off a log**

  Meaning: Something very easy or simple to do is as easy as falling off a log.

- **Easy as pie**

  Meaning: If something is easy as pie, it is very easy indeed.
- **Easy come, easy go**

  Meaning: This idiom means that money or other material gains that come without much effort tend to get spent or consumed as easily.
- **Easy does it**

  Meaning: 'Easy does it' is used to advise someone to approach a task carefully and slowly, especially in spoken English.
- **Easy peasy**

  Meaning: If something is easy peasy, it is very easy indeed.
- **Eat humble pie**

  Meaning: If someone apologises and shows a lot of contrition for something they have done, they eat humble pie.
- **Eat like a bird**

  Meaning: If someone eats like a bird, they eat very little.
- **Eat like a horse**

  Meaning: Someone who eats like a horse, eats a lot.
- **Eat like a pig**

  Meaning: If some eats like a pig, they either eat too much or they have bad table manners.
- **Eat someone alive**

  Meaning: If you eat someone alive, you defeat or beat them comprehensively.
- **Eat your heart out**

  Meaning: If someone tells you to eat your heart out, they are saying they are better than you at something.
- **Eat your words**

  Meaning: If you eat your words, you accept publicly that you were wrong about something you said.
- **Egg on your face**

  Meaning: If someone has egg on their face, they are made to look foolish or embarrassed.

- **Elbow grease**
  Meaning: If something requires elbow grease, it involves a lot of hard physical work.
- **Elbow room**
  Meaning: If you haven't got enough elbow room, you haven't got enough space.
- **Elephant in the room**
  Meaning: An elephant in the room is a problem that everyone knows very well but no one talks about because it is taboo, embarrassing, etc.
- **Elephant has two set of teeth-one to show off and the other to chew with**
  Meaning: What you see is not necessarily true.
- **Eleventh hour**
  Meaning: If something happens at the eleventh hour, it happens right at the last minute.
- **Embarrassed cat scratches a pillar**
  Meaning: To be embarrassed.
- **Empty vessels make the most noise**
  Meaning: The thoughtless often speak the most.
- **Etched in stone**
  Meaning: Something, especially rules and customs, that cannot be changed at all is said to be etched in stone.
- **Even a blind squirrel finds a nut once in a while**
  Meaning: This expression means that even if people are ineffective or misguided, sometimes they can still be correct just by being lucky.
- **Even a broken clock is right twice a day**
  Meaning: This is used when people get lucky and are undeservedly successful.
- **Even Stevens**
  Meaning: If everything is equal between people, they are even Stevens.
- **Even the dogs in the street know**
  Meaning: This idiom is used frequently in Ireland, and means

something is so obvious that even the dogs in the street know it.

- **Every ass likes to hear himself bray**

  Meaning: This means that people like the sound of their own voice.

- **Every dog has its day**

  Meaning: This idiom means that everyone gets their moment to shine.

- **Every man and his dog**

  Meaning: A lot of people – as in sending out invitations to a large number of people

- **Every man for himself**

  Meaning: If it's every man for himself, then people are trying to save themselves from a difficult situation without trying to help anyone else.

- **Every man has his price**

  Meaning: Anyone's opinion or support can be bought, everyone's principles have a limit.

- **Every man jack**

  Meaning: If every man jack was involved in something, it is an emphatic way of saying that absolutely everybody was involved.

- **Every nook and cranny**

  Meaning: If you search every nook and cranny, you look everywhere for something.

- **Every trick in the book**

  Meaning: If you try every trick in the book, you try every possible way, including dishonesty and deceit, to get what you want.

- **Everybody and their uncle**

  Meaning: This basically means a lot of people or too many people; everybody and their uncle was there.

- **Everything but the kitchen sink**

  Meaning: If people include everything but the kitchen sink, they include every possibility, regardless of whether they are useful.

- **Explore all avenues**

  Meaning: If all avenues are being explored, then every conceivable approach is being tried that could possibly get the desired result.

- **Eye candy**

  Meaning: When a person is very attractive, they can be described as eye candy – sweet to look at!

- **Eye for an eye**

  Meaning: This is an expression for retributive justice, where the punishment equals the crime.

- **Eye-opener**

  Meaning: Something surprising, unexpected which reveals the truth about something or someone.

- **Eyes are bigger than one's stomach**

  Meaning: If someone's eyes are bigger than their stomach, they are greedy and take on more than they can consume or manage.

F

- **Face like thunder**

  Meaning: If someone has a face like thunder, they are clearly very angry or upset about something.

- **Face only a mother could love**

  Meaning: When someone has a face only a mother could love, they are ugly.

- **Face the music**

  Meaning: If you have to face the music, you have to accept the negative consequences of something you have done wrong.

- **Face value**

  Meaning: If you take something at face value, you accept the appearance rather than looking deeper into the matter.

- **Face your demons**

  Meaning: If you face your demons, you confront your fears or something that you have been trying hard to avoid.

- **Facts of life**

  Meaning: When someone is taught the facts of life, they learn about sex and reproduction.

- **Failure is the mother of success**

  Meaning: Failure is often a stepping stone towards success.

- **Faint heart never won fair lady**

  Meaning: This means that you will not get the partner of your dreams if you lack the confidence to let them know how you feel.

- **Fair and square**

  Meaning: If someone does something fair and square, they do it correctly, following any rules or laws.

- **Fair crack of the whip**

  Meaning: If everybody has a fair crack of the whip, they all have equal opportunities to do something.

- **Fair game**

  Meaning: If something or someone is fair game, then it is acceptable to target, criticise or attack them.

- **Fair shake of the whip**

  Meaning: If everybody has a fair shake of the whip, they all have equal opportunities to do something.

- **Fall at the first fence**

  Meaning: If something falls at the first fence, it goes wrong or fails at the first or an early stage.

- **Fall at the first hurdle**

  Meaning: If something falls at the first hurdle, it goes wrong or fails at the first or an early stage.

- **Fall by the wayside**

  Meaning: To fall by the wayside is to give up or fail before completion.

- **Fall from grace**

  Meaning: If a person falls from grace, they lose favour with someone.

- **Fall off the back of a lorry**

  Meaning: If someone tries to sell you something that has fallen of the back of a lorry, they are trying to sell you stolen goods.

- **Fall off the turnip truck**

  Meaning: If someone has just fallen off the turnip truck, they are uninformed, naive and gullible.

- **Fall off the wagon**

  Meaning: If someone falls off the wagon, they start drinking after having given up completely for a time.

- **Fall on our feet**

  Meaning: If you fall on your feet, you succeed in doing something where there was a risk of failure.

- **Fall on stony ground**

  Meaning: If an idea or plan falls on stony ground, it is received negatively by people in positions of power or fails to take-off.

- **Fall on your sword**

  Meaning: If someone falls on their sword, they resign or accept the consequences of some wrongdoing.

- **Familiarity breeds contempt**

  Meaning: This means that the more you know something or someone, the more you start to find faults and dislike things about it or them.

- **Far cry from**

  Meaning: This means that something is very different from something.

- **Fast and furious**

  Meaning: Things that happen fast and furious happen very quickly without stopping or pausing.

- **Fat cat**

  Meaning: A fat cat is a person who makes a lot of money and enjoys a privileged position in society.

- **Fat chance!**

  Meaning: This idiom is a way of telling someone they have no chance.
- **Fat head**

  Meaning: A fat head is a dull, stupid person.
- **Fat hits the fire**

  Meaning: When the fat hits the fire, trouble breaks out.
- **Fat of the land**

  Meaning: Living off the fat of the land means having the best of everything in life.
- **Fate worse than death**

  Meaning: Describing something as a fate worse than death is a fairly common way of implying that it is unpleasant.
- **Father figure**

  Meaning: A father figure is an older man, often in a position of power or authority, who commands great respect and inspires feelings like those for a father.
- **Feather in your cap**

  Meaning: A success or achievement that may help you in the future is a feather in your cap.
- **Feather your own nest**

  Meaning: If someone feathers their own nest, they use their position or job for personal gain.
- **Feathers fly**

  Meaning: When people are fighting or arguing angrily, we can say that feathers are flying.
- **Fed up to the back teeth**

  Meaning: When you are extremely irritated and fed up with something or someone, you are fed up to the back teeth.
- **Feel at home**

  Meaning: If you feel relaxed and comfortable somewhere or with someone, you feel at home.
- **Feel free**

  Meaning: If you ask for permission to do something and are told to feel free, the other person means that there is absolutely no problem

- **Feel the pinch**

  Meaning: If someone is short of money or feeling restricted in some other way, they are feeling the pinch.
- **Feeling blue**

  Meaning: If you feel blue, you are feeling unwell, mainly associated with depression or unhappiness.
- **Feet of clay**

  Meaning: If someone has feet of clay, they have flaws that make them seem more human and like normal people.
- **Fence sitter**

  Meaning: Someone that tries to support both side of an argument without committing to either is a fence sitter.
- **Fever pitch**

  Meaning: When a situation has reached fever pitch, people are extremely excited or agitated.
- **Few and far between**

  Meaning: If things are few and far between, they happen very occasionally.
- **Fifth columnist**

  Meaning: A fifth columnist is a member of a subversive organization who tries to help an enemy invade.
- **Fifth wheel**

  Meaning: A fifth wheel is something unnecessary or useless.
- **Fight an uphill battle**

  Meaning: When you fight an uphill battle, you have to struggle against very unfavourable circumstances.
- **Fight tooth and nail**

  Meaning: If someone will fight tooth and nail for something, they will not stop at anything to get what they want.
- **Fighting chance**

  Meaning: If you have a fighting chance, you have a reasonable possibility of success.

- **Find your feet**

  Meaning: When you are finding your feet, you are in the process of gaining confidence and experience in something.

- **Finders keepers, losers weepers**

  Meaning: Whoever finds something can keep it. This is often shortened to 'finders keepers'.

- **Fine and dandy**

  Meaning: If things are fine and dandy, then everything is going well.

- **Fine tuning**

  Meaning: Small adjustments to improve something or to get it working are called fine tuning.

- **Fine words butter no parsnips**

  Meaning: This idiom means that it's easy to talk, but talk is not action.

- **Finger in the pie**

  Meaning: If you have a finger in the pie, you have an interest in something.

- **Fingers and thumbs**

  Meaning: If you are all fingers and thumbs, you are being clumsy and not very skilled with your hands.

- **Fire away**

  Meaning: If you want to ask someone a question and they tell you to fire away, they mean that you are free to ask what you want.

- **Fire in the hole!**

  Meaning: This is used as a warning when a planned explosion is about to happen.

- **Fire on all cylinders**

  Meaning: If something is firing on all cylinders, it is going as well as it could.

- **First come, first served**

  Meaning: This means there will be no preferential treatment and a service will be provided to those that arrive first.

- **First out of the gate**

  Meaning: When someone is first out of the gate, they are the first to do something that others are trying to do.
- **First port of call**

  Meaning: The first place you stop to do something is your first port of call.
- **Fish or cut bait**

  Meaning: This idiom is used when you want to tell someone that it is time to take action.
- **Fish out of water**

  Meaning: If you are placed in a situation that is completely new to you and confuses you, you are like a fish out of water.
- **Fishy**

  Meaning: If there is something fishy about someone or something, there is something suspicious; a feeling that there is something wrong, though it isn't clear what it is.
- **Fit as a butcher's dog**

  Meaning: Someone who's very healthy, fit or physically attractive is as fit as a butcher's dog.
- **Fit as a fiddle**

  Meaning: If you are fit as a fiddle, you are in perfect health.
- **Fit for a king**

  Meaning: If something is fit for a king, it is of the very highest quality or standard.
- **Fit like a glove**

  Meaning: If something fits like a glove, it is suitable or the right size.
- **Fit of pique**

  Meaning: If someone reacts badly because their pride is hurt, this is a fit of pique.
- **Fit the bill**

  Meaning: If something fits the bill, it is what is required for the task.

- **Fit to be tied**

  Meaning: If someone is fit to be tied, they are extremely angry.
- **Five o'clock shadow**

  Meaning: A five o'clock shadow is the facial hair that a man gets if he doesn't shave for a day or two.
- **Flowery speech**

  Meaning: Flowery speech is full of lovely words, but may well lack substance.
- **Flutter the dovecotes**

  Meaning: Something that flutters the dovecots causes alarm or excitement.
- **Fly in the ointment**

  Meaning: A fly in the ointment is something that spoils or prevents complete enjoyment of something.
- **Fly off the handle**

  Meaning: If someone flies off the handle, they get very angry.
- **Fly on the wall**

  Meaning: If you are able to see and hear events as they happen, you are a fly on the wall.
- **Fly the coop**

  Meaning: When children leave home to live away from their parents, they fly the coop.
- **Fly the flag**

  Meaning: If someone flies the flag, they represent or support their country.
- **Foam at the mouth**

  Meaning: If you foam at the mouth, you are very, very angry.
- **Follow your nose**

  Meaning: When giving directions, telling someone to follow their nose means that they should go straight ahead.
- **Food for thought**

  Meaning: If something is food for thought, it is worth thinking about or considering seriously.

- **Fool me once, shame on you; fool me twice, shame on me**

  Meaning: This means that you should learn from your mistakes and not allow people to take advantage of you repeatedly.
- **Fool's paradise**

  Meaning: A fool's paradise is a false sense of happiness or success.
- **Fools rush in where angels fear to tread**

  Meaning: This idiom is used where people who are inexperienced or lack knowledge do something that more informed people would avoid.
- **Foot in mouth**

  Meaning: This is used to describe someone who has just said something embarrassing, inappropriate, wrong or stupid.
- **Foot the bill**

  Meaning: The person who foots the bill pays the bill for everybody.
- **For a song**

  Meaning: If you buy or sell something for a song, it is very cheap.
- **For donkey's years**

  Meaning: If people have done something, usually without much if any change, for an awfully long time, they can be said to have done it for donkey's years.
- **For kicks**

  Meaning: If you do something for kicks, or just for kicks, you do it purely for fun or thrills.
- **For my money**

  Meaning: This idiom means 'in my opinion'.
- **For the birds**

  Meaning: If something is worthless or ridiculous, it is for the birds.
- **For the time being**

  Meaning: For the time being indicates that an action or state will continue into the future, but is temporary. I'm sharing an office for the time being.

- **Forbidden fruit**

  Meaning: Something enjoyable that is illegal or immoral is forbidden fruit.
- **Foregone conclusion**

  Meaning: If the result of, say, a football match is a foregone conclusion, then the result is obvious before the game has even begun.
- **Forest for the trees**

  Meaning: If someone can't see the forest for the trees, they get so caught up in small details that they fail to understand the bigger picture.
- **Fortune knocks once at every man's door**

  Meaning: Everyone gets one good chance in a lifetime.
- **Foul play**

  Meaning: If the police suspect foul play, they think a crime was committed.
- **Four corners of the earth**

  Meaning: If something goes to, or comes from, the four corners of the earth, it goes or comes absolutely everywhere.
- **Four-eyes**

  Meaning: A person who wears glasses
- **Four-square behind**

  Meaning: If someone stands four-square behind someone, they give that person their full support.
- **Fourth estate**

  Meaning: This is an idiomatic way of describing the media, especially the newspapers.
- **Free-for-all**

  Meaning: A free-for-all is a fight or contest in which everyone gets involved and rules are not respected.
- **French leave**

  Meaning: To take French leave is to leave a gathering without saying goodbye or without permission.

- **Fresh from the oven**

  Meaning: If something is fresh from the oven, it is very new.
- **Friendly footing**

  Meaning: When relationships are on a friendly footing, they are going well.
- **Frog in my throat**

  Meaning: If you have a frog in your throat, you can't speak or you are losing your voice because you have a problem with your throat.
- **From a different angle**

  Meaning: If you look at something from a different angle, you look at it from a different point of view.
- **From Missouri**

  Meaning: If someone is from Missouri, then they require clear proof before they will believe something.
- **From pillar to post**

  Meaning: If something is going from pillar to post, it is moving around in a meaningless way, from one disaster to another.
- **From rags to riches**

  Meaning: Someone who starts life very poor and makes a fortune goes from rags to riches.
- **From scratch**

  Meaning: This idiom means 'from the beginning'.
- **From soup to nuts**

  Meaning: If you do something from soup to nuts, you do it from the beginning right to the very end.
- **From the bottom of your heart**

  Meaning: If someone does something from the bottom of their heart, then they do it with genuine emotion and feeling.
- **From the get-go**

  Meaning: From the very beginning.
- **From the horse's mouth**

  Meaning: If you hear something from the horse's mouth,

you hear it directly from the person concerned or responsible.

- **From the sublime to the ridiculous**

  Meaning: If something declines considerably in quality or importance, it is said to have gone from the sublime to the ridiculous.

- **From the word go**

  Meaning: From the word go means from the very beginning of something.

- **From your lips to God's ears**

  Meaning: When you say this to someone, it means that you hope what they are saying will come true.

- **Full as a tick**

  Meaning: If you are as full as a tick, you have eaten too much.

- **Full bore**

  Meaning: If something is full bore, it involves the maximum effort or is complete and thorough.

- **Full circle**

  Meaning: When something has come full circle, it has ended up where it started.

- **Full Monty**

  Meaning: If something is the Full Monty, it is the real thing, not reduced in any way.

- **Full of beans**

  Meaning: If someone's full of beans, they are very energetic.

- **Full of hot air**

  Meaning: Someone who is full of hot air talks a lot of rubbish.

- **Full of oneself**

  Meaning: Someone who acts in an arrogant or egotistical manner is full of himself/herself.

- **Full of piss and vinegar**

  Meaning: Someone who's full of piss and vinegar is full of youthful energy.

- **Full of the joys of spring**

  Meaning: If you are full of the joys of spring, you are very happy and full of energy.

- **Full speed ahead**

  Meaning: If people do something with all their enthusiasm and energy, they go full speed ahead.

- **Full swing**

  Meaning: If a something is in full swing, it is going or doing well.

- **Full throttle**

  Meaning: If you do something full throttle, you do it with as much speed and energy as you can.

- **Fullness of time**

  Meaning: If something happens in the fullness of time, it will happen when the time is right and appropriate.

- **Fur coat and no knickers**

  Meaning: Someone with airs and graces, but no real class is fur coat and no knickers.

- **Fuzzy thinking**

  Meaning: Thinking or ideas that do not agree with the facts or information available

G

- **Game on**

  Meaning: When someone says 'Game on!', it means that they are accepting a challenge or ready to get something done.

- **Game plan**

  Meaning: A game plan is a strategy.

- **Ganga flows backwards**

  Meaning: To go against the law of nature.

- **Garbage fee**

  Meaning: A garbage fee is a charge that has no value and doesn't provide any real service.

- **Garbage in, garbage out**

  Meaning: If a computer system or database is built badly, then the results will be bad.

- **Gather pace**

  Meaning: If events gather pace, they move faster.

- **Gather steam**

  Meaning: If something gathers speed, it moves or progresses at an increasing speed.

- **Get a grip**

  Meaning: If you get a grip, you control your emotions so that they don't overwhelm you.

- **Get a handle on**

  Meaning: When you get a handle on something, you come to understand it.

- **Get along famously**

  Meaning: If people get along famously, they have an exceedingly good relationship.

- **Get away scot-free**

  Meaning: If someone gets away scot-free, they are not punished when they have done something wrong.

- **Get away with murder**

  Meaning: If you get away with murder, you do something bad and don't get caught or punished.

- **Get cracking**

  Meaning: To get cracking means to start working on something, usually a job or task with defined parameters.

- **Get in on the act**

  Meaning: If people want to get in on the act, they want to participate in something that is currently profitable or popular.

- **Get in on the ground floor**

  Meaning: If you get in on the ground floor, you enter a project or venture at the start before people know how successful it might be.

- **Get it in the neck**

  Meaning: If you get it in the neck, you are punished or criticised for something.

- **Get it off your chest**

  Meaning: If you get something off your chest, you confess to something that has been troubling you.

- **Get my drift**

  Meaning: If you get someone's drift, you understand what they are trying to say.

- **Get off the ground**

  Meaning: If a project or plan gets off the ground, it starts to be put into operation.

- **Get on like a house on fire**

  Meaning: If people get on like a house on fire, they have a very close and good relationship.

- **Get on your nerves**

  Meaning: If something gets on your nerves, it annoys or irritates you.

- **Get out of bed on the wrong side**

  Meaning: If you get out of bed on the wrong side, you wake up and start the day in a bad mood for no real reason.

- **Get out of your pram**

  Meaning: If someone gets out of their pram, they respond aggressively to an argument or problem that doesn't involve them.

- **Get the axe**

  Meaning: If you get the axe, you lose your job.

- **Get the ball rolling**

  Meaning: If you get the ball rolling, you start something so that it can start making progress.

- **Get the green light**

  Meaning: If you get the green light to do something, you are given the necessary permission, authorization.

- **Get the hang of it**

  Meaning: When you get the hang of something, you are familiar with it and know how to do it.
- **Get the lead out**

  Meaning: This is used to tell someone to hurry up.
- **Get the monkey off your back**

  Meaning: If you get the monkey off your back, you pass on a problem to someone else.
- **Get the nod**

  Meaning: If you get the nod to something, you get approval or permission to do it.
- **Get the picture**

  Meaning: If you get the picture, you understand a situation fully.
- **Get the show on the road**

  Meaning: If you get the show on the road, you put a plan into operation or begin something.
- **Get to grips**

  Meaning: If you get to grips with something, you take control and do it properly.
- **Get up and go**

  Meaning: If someone has lots of get up and go, they have lots of enthusiasm and energy.
- **Get wind of**

  Meaning: If you get wind of something, you hear or learn about it, especially if it was meant to be secret.
- **Get your ducks in a row**

  Meaning: If you get your ducks in a row, you organise yourself and your life.
- **Get your feathers in a bunch**

  Meaning: If you get your feathers in a bunch, you get upset or angry about something.
- **Get your feet wet**

  Meaning: If you get your feet wet, you gain your first experience of something.

- **Get your goat**

  Meaning: If something gets your goat, it annoys you.
- **Get your head around something**

  Meaning: If you get your head around something, you come to understand it even though it is difficult to comprehend.
- **Get your skates on**

  Meaning: This is used as a way of telling people to hurry up.
- **Get your teeth into**

  Meaning: If you get your teeth into something, you become involved in or do something that is intellectually challenging or satisfying.
- **Get your wires crossed**

  Meaning: If people get their wires cross, they misunderstand each other, especially when making arrangements.
- **Ghost of a chance**

  Meaning: If something or someone hasn't got a ghost of a chance, they have no hope whatsoever of succeeding.
- **Ghostly presence**

  Meaning: You can feel or otherwise sense a ghostly presence, but you cannot do it clearly only vaguely.
- **Gift of the gab**

  Meaning: If someone has the gift of the gab, they speak in a persuasive and interesting way.
- **Gild the lily**

  Meaning: If you gild the lily, you decorate something that is already ornate.
- **Girl Friday**

  Meaning: A girl Friday is a female employee who assists someone without any specific duties.
- **Give a big hand**

  Meaning: Applaud by clapping hands. 'Let's give all the contestants a big hand.'
- **Give and take**

  Meaning: Where there is give and take, people make concessions in order to get things they want in negotiations.

- **Give as good as you get**

  Meaning: If you give as good as you get, you are prepared to treat people as badly as they treat you and to fight for what you believe.

- **Give away the store**

  Meaning: If someone gives away the store, they say or do something that makes their position in negotiations, debates, etc., much weaker.

- **Give it some stick**

  Meaning: If you give something some stick, you put a lot of effort into it.

- **Give me a hand**

  Meaning: If someone gives you a hand, they help you.

- **Give me five**

  Meaning: If someone says this, they want to hit your open hand against theirs as a way of congratulation or greeting.

- **Give someone a leg up**

  Meaning: If you give someone a leg up, you help them to achieve something that they couldn't have done alone.

- **Give someone a piece of your mind**

  Meaning: If you give someone a piece of your mind, you criticise them strongly and angrily.

- **Give someone a run for their money**

  Meaning: If you can give someone a run for the money, you are as good, or nearly as good, as they are at something.

- **Give someone enough rope**

  Meaning: If you give someone enough rope, you give them the chance to get themselves into trouble or expose themselves.

- **Give someone stick**

  Meaning: If someone gives you stick, they criticise you or punish you.

- **Give someone the run around**

  Meaning: If someone gives you the runaround, they make excuses and give you false explanations to avoid doing something.

- **Give the nod**

  Meaning: If you give the nod to something, you approve it or give permission to do it.
- **Give up the ghost**

  Meaning: People give up the ghost when they die. Machines stop working when they give up the ghost.
- **Give your eye teeth**

  Meaning: If you really want something and would be prepared to sacrifice a lot to get it, you would give your eye teeth for it.
- **Glass ceiling**

  Meaning: The glass ceiling is the discrimination that prevents women and minorities from getting promoted to the highest levels of companies and organizations.
- **Glimmer of hope**

  Meaning: A glimmer of hope is the belief that there is a slight chance that something positive will happen.
- **Glory hound**

  Meaning: A glory hound is a person seeking popularity, fame and glory.
- **Gnaw your vitals**

  Meaning: If something gnaws your vitals, it troubles you greatly and affects you at a very deep level.
- **Go awry**

  Meaning: If things go awry, they go wrong.
- **Go bananas**

  Meaning: If you go bananas, you are wild with excitement, anxiety, or worry.
- **Go blue**

  Meaning: If you go blue, you are very cold indeed.
- **Go bust**

  Meaning: If a company goes bust, it goes bankrupt.
- **Go by the board**

  Meaning: When something has gone by the board, it no longer exists or an opportunity has been lost.

- **Go by the boards**

  Meaning: If something goes by the boards, it fails to get approved or accepted.
- **Go down a storm**

  Meaning: To say that something has been enjoyable or successful, you can say that it has gone down a storm.
- **Go down like a cup of cold sick**

  Meaning: An idea or excuse that will not be well accepted will go down like a cup of cold sick.
- **Go down like a lead balloon**

  Meaning: If something goes down like a lead balloon, it fails or is extremely badly received.
- **Go down swinging**

  Meaning: If you want to go down swinging, you know you will probably fail, but you refuse to give up.
- **Go down without a fight**

  Meaning: If someone goes down without a fight, they surrender without putting up any resistance.
- **Go Dutch**

  Meaning: If you go Dutch in a restaurant, you pay equal shares for the meal.
- **Go fly a kite**

  Meaning: This is used to tell someone to go away and leave you alone.
- **Go for broke**

  Meaning: If someone goes for broke, they risk everything they have for a potentially greater gain.
- **Go for the jugular**

  Meaning: If you go for the jugular, you attack someone where they are most vulnerable.
- **Go fry an egg**

  Meaning: This is used to tell someone to go away and leave you alone.

- **Go hand in hand**
  Meaning: If things go hand in hand, they are associated and go together.
- **Go haywire**
  Meaning: When something goes haywire, it is completely out of control and erratic.
- **Go nuts**
  Meaning: If someone goes nuts, they get excited over something.
- **Go off on a tangent**
  Meaning: If someone goes off on a tangent, they change the subject completely in the middle of a conversation or talk.
- **Go overboard**
  Meaning: If you go overboard, you do something excessively.
- **Go pear-shaped**
  Meaning: If things have gone wrong, they have gone pear-shaped.
- **Go play in traffic**
  Meaning: This is used as a way of telling someone to go away.
- **Go south**
  Meaning: If things go south, they get worse or go wrong.
- **Go spare**
  Meaning: If you go spare, you lose your temper completely.
- **Go tell it to birds**
  Meaning: This is used when someone says something that is not credible or is a lie.
- **Go the distance**
  Meaning: If you go the distance, you continue until something ends, no matter how difficult.
- **Go the whole hog**
  Meaning: If you go the whole hog, you do something completely or to its limits.
- **Go through the motions**
  Meaning: When you go through the motions, you do

something like an everyday routine and without any feelings whatsoever.

- **Go to the mat**

  Meaning: If people go to the mat, they continue to struggle or fight to the end, until they have either won or have finally been defeated.

- **Go to seed**

  Meaning: If someone has gone to seed, they have declined in quality or appearance.

- **Go to the wall**

  Meaning: If a company goes to the wall, it goes bust or fails.

- **Go to the wire**

  Meaning: If someone goes to the wire, they risk their life, job, reputation, etc., to help someone.

- **Go to your head**

  Meaning: If something goes to your head, it makes you feel vain. If alcohol goes to your head, it makes you feel drunk quickly.

- **Go under the hammer**

  Meaning: If something goes under the hammer, it is sold in an auction.

- **Go west**

  Meaning: If something goes west, it goes wrong. If someone goes west, they die.

- **Go with the flow**

  Meaning: If you go with the flow, you accept things as they happen and do what everyone else wants to do.

- **God made match, one is blind and the other is a leper**

  Meaning: Made for each other in a negative manner.

- **Going concern**

  Meaning: A successful and active business is a going concern.

- **Going Jesse**

  Meaning: If something is a going Jesse, it's a viable, successful project or enterprise.

- **Going overboard**

  Meaning: If you go overboard with something, then you take something too far, or do too much.
- **Golden handshake**

  Meaning: A golden handshake is a payment made to someone to get them to leave their job.
- **Golden opportunity**

  Meaning: A golden opportunity is usually a good chance to do or succeed at something. A chance that should not be missed.
- **Golden touch**

  Meaning: Someone with a golden touch can make money from or be successful at anything they do.
- **Gone fishing**

  Meaning: If someone has gone fishing, they are not very aware of what is happening around them.
- **Gone for a Burton**

  Meaning: If something's gone for a Burton, it has been spoiled or ruined. If a person has gone for a burton, they are either in serious trouble or have died.
- **Gone pear-shaped**

  Meaning: If things have gone pear-shaped they have either gone wrong or produced an unexpected and unwanted result.
- **Gone time does not come back**

  Meaning: Don't dwell in past; Time doesn't come back so no point wasting time.
- **Gone to pot**

  Meaning: If something has gone to pot, it has gone wrong and doesn't work anymore.
- **Gone to the dogs**

  Meaning: If something has gone to the dogs, it has gone badly wrong and lost all the good things it had.
- **Good antennae**

  Meaning: Someone with good antennae is good at detecting things.

- **Good as gold**

  Meaning: If children are as good as gold, they behave very well.
- **Good egg**

  Meaning: A person who can be relied on is a good egg. Bad egg is the opposite.
- **Good hand**

  Meaning: If you are a good hand at something, you do it well.
- **Good offices**

  Meaning: Good offices is help and support, especially in mediating in a dispute.
- **Good person sees the whole world as good**

  Meaning: Good person sees the whole world as good.
- **Good Samaritan**

  Meaning: A good Samaritan is a person who helps others in need.
- **Good shape**

  Meaning: If something's in good shape, it's in good condition. If a person's in good shape, they are fit and healthy.
- **Good time**

  Meaning: If you make good time on a journey, you manage to travel faster than you expected.
- **Good to go**

  Meaning: Someone or something that meets one's approval. 'He is good to go.' 'The idea you had is good to go.'
- **Good walls make good neighbours**

  Meaning: Your relationship with your neighbours depends, among other things, on respecting one another's privacy.
- **Goody two-shoes**

  Meaning: A goody two-shoes is a self-righteous person who makes a great deal of their virtue.
- **Grab the bull by its horns**

  Meaning: If you grab the bull by its horns, you deal head-on and directly with a problem.

- **Grapes are sour**

  Meaning: Disparagement of something that is unattainable.
- **Grasp the nettle**

  Meaning: If you grasp the nettle, you deal bravely with a problem.
- **Grass roots**

  Meaning: This idiom is often used in politics, where it refers to the ordinary people or voters. It can be used to mean people at the bottom of a hierarchy.
- **Graveyard shift**

  Meaning: If you have to work very late at night, it is the graveyard shift.
- **Gravy train**

  Meaning: If someone is on the gravy train, they have found and easy way to make lots of money.
- **Grease monkey**

  Meaning: A grease monkey is an idiomatic term for a mechanic.
- **Grease someone's palm**

  Meaning: If you grease someone's palm, you bribe them to do something.
- **Grease the skids**

  Meaning: If you grease the skids, you facilitate something.
- **Greased lightning**

  Meaning: If something or someone moves like greased lightning, they move very fast indeed.
- **Great guns**

  Meaning: If something or someone is going great guns, they are doing very well.
- **Great minds think alike**

  Meaning: If two people have the same thought at the same time, one of them might say "Great minds think alike."
- **Great Scott**

  Meaning: An exclamation of surprise.

- **Great unwashed**

  Meaning: This is a term used for the working class masses.
- **Great white hope**

  Meaning: Someone who is expected to be a great success is a great white hope.
- **Greek to me**

  Meaning: If you don't understand something, it's all Greek to you.
- **Green around the gills**

  Meaning: If someone looks green around the gills, they look ill.
- **Green fingers**

  Meaning: Someone with green fingers has a talent for gardening.
- **Green light**

  Meaning: If you are given the green light, you are given approval to do something.
- **Green thumb**

  Meaning: Someone with a talent for gardening has a green thumb.
- **Green with envy**

  Meaning: If you are green with envy, you are very jealous.
- **Green-eyed monster**

  Meaning: The green-eyed monster is an allegorical phrase for somebody's strong jealousy.
- **Greenhorn**

  Meaning: A greenhorn or someone who is described simply as green lacks the relevant experience and knowledge for their job or task.
- **Grey area**

  Meaning: A grey/gray area is one where there is no clear right or wrong.
- **Grey Cardinal**

  Meaning: Someone who is a Grey Cardinal exerts power behind the scenes, without drawing attention to himself or herself.

- **Grey cells**

  Meaning: 'Grey cells' means 'brain'.

- **Grey matter**

  Meaning: Grey/gray matter is the human brain.

- **Grey suits**

  Meaning: The men in grey suits are people who have a lot of power in business or politics, but aren't well-known or charismatic.

- **Grin and bear it**

  Meaning: If you have to grin and bear it, you have to accept something that you don't like.

- **Grin like a Cheshire cat**

  Meaning: If someone has a very wide smile, they have a grin like a Cheshire cat.

- **Grinds my gear**

  Meaning: Something that is very annoying grinds your gear.

- **Grist for the mill**

  Meaning: Something that you can use to your advantage is grist for the mill.

- **Grow in the telling**

  Meaning: The more you tell it, the larger, wilder, better, etc. the story gets.

- **Guinea-pig**

  Meaning: If you are a guinea-pig, you take part in an experiment of some sort and are used in the testing.

- **Gunboat diplomacy**

  Meaning: If a nation conducts its diplomatic relations by threatening military action to get what it wants, it is using gunboat diplomacy.

- **Gung ho**

  Meaning: If someone is gung ho about something, they support it blindly and don't think about the consequences.

H

- **Hail-fellow-well-met**

  Meaning: Someone whose behaviour is hearty, friendly and congenial.

- **Hairy at the heel**

  Meaning: Someone who is hairy at the heel is dangerous or untrustworthy.

- **Hale and hearty**

  Meaning: Someone who is hale and hearty is in very good health.

- **Half a loaf is better than no bread**

  Meaning: It means that getting part of what you want is better than getting nothing at all.

- **Half a mind**

  Meaning: If you have half a mind to do something, you haven't decided to do it, but are thinking seriously about doing it.

- **Half-baked**

  Meaning: A half-baked idea or scheme hasn't not been thought through or planned very well.

- **Hand in glove**

  Meaning: If people are hand in glove, they have an extremely close relationship.

- **Hand that rocks the cradle**

  Meaning: Women have a great power and influence because they have the greatest influence over the development of children- the hand that rocks the cradle.

- **Hand to mouth**

  Meaning: Someone who's living from hand to mouth, is very poor and needs the little money they have coming in to cover their expenses.

- **Hands down**

  Meaning: If someone is better hands down than everyone else, they are much better.

- **Handwriting like chicken scratch**

  Meaning: If your handwriting is very hard to read, it is like chicken scratch.
- **Hang by a thread**

  Meaning: If something hangs by a thread, there is a very small chance indeed of it being successful or surviving.
- **Hang in the balance**

  Meaning: If an outcome is hanging in the balance, there are at least two possibilities and it is impossible to predict which will win out.
- **Hang out to dry**

  Meaning: If you hang someone out to dry, you abandon them when they are in trouble.
- **Happy as Larry**

  Meaning: When you're as happy as Larry, you're very happy indeed.
- **Happy medium**

  Meaning: If you reach a happy medium, you are making a compromise; reaching a conclusion or decision.
- **Happy-go-lucky**

  Meaning: If someone is happy-go-lucky, they don't worry or plan and accept things as they happen.
- **Hard act to follow**

  Meaning: If something or something is exceptionally good, it is difficult to replace them or take their place.
- **Hard as nails**

  Meaning: A person who is as hard as nails is either physically tough or has little or no respect for other people's feelings.
- **Hard cheese**

  Meaning: Hard cheese means hard luck.
- **Hard of hearing**

  Meaning: Someone who's hard of hearing is a bit deaf.

- **Hard sell**
  Meaning: If someone puts a lot of pressure on you to do or buy something, they are hard selling it.
- **Hard to come by**
  Meaning: If something is hard to come by, it is difficult to find.
- **Hard up**
  Meaning: If you are hard up, you have very little money.
- **Hat trick**
  Meaning: Three successes one after the other is a hat trick.
- **Hatchet job**
  Meaning: A piece of criticism that destroys someone's reputation is a hatchet job.
- **Haul someone over the coals**
  Meaning: If you haul someone over the coals, you reprimand them severely.
- **Have a ball**
  Meaning: If you have a ball, you have a great time, a lot of fun.
- **Have a bash**
  Meaning: If you have a bash at something, you try to do it, especially when there isn't much chance of success.
- **Have a blast**
  Meaning: It means to have a lot of fun.
- **Have a foot in both camps**
  Meaning: Someone who plays a part or who is involved in two different groups of people, opinions, ways of thinking or living, etc., has a foot in both camps.
- **Have a go**
  Meaning: If you have a go, you try to do something, often when you don't think you have much chance of succeeding.
- **Have a ripper**
  Meaning: If you have a ripper of a time, you enjoy yourself.
- **Have a trick up your sleeve**
  Meaning: If you have a trick up your sleeve, you have a secret strategy to use when the time is right.

- **Have no truck with**

  Meaning: If you have no truck with something or someone, you refuse to get involved with it or them.
- **Have someone in your corner**

  Meaning: If you have someone in your corner, you have their support or help.
- **Have something up your sleeve**

  Meaning: If you have something up your sleeve, you have some hidden or secret plan, idea, etc., to use to your advantage when the time is right.
- **Have the floor**

  Meaning: If someone has the floor, it is their turn to speak at a meeting.
- **Have the guts**

  Meaning: Someone who has enough courage.
- **Have your cake and eat it too**

  Meaning: If someone wants to have their cake and eat it too, they want everything their way, especially when their wishes are contradictory.
- **Have your collar felt**

  Meaning: If someone has their collar felt, they are arrested.
- **Have your fill**

  Meaning: If you have had your fill, you are fed up of somebody or something.
- **Have your lunch handed to you**

  Meaning: If you have you lunch handed to you, you are outperformed and shown up by someone better.
- **Have your moments**

  Meaning: Someone who has his or her moments exhibits a positive behaviour pattern on an occasional basis but not generally.
- **Have your tail up**

  Meaning: If someone has their tail up, they are optimistic and expect to be successful.

- **Have your work cut out**

  Meaning: If you have your work cut out, you are very busy indeed.
- **Having a gas**

  Meaning: If you're having a gas, you are having a laugh and enjoying yourself in company.
- **Hay is for horses**

  Meaning: This idiom is used as a way of telling children not to say the word 'hey' as in hey you or hey there.
- **Head for the hills**

  Meaning: If people head for the hills, they run away from trouble.
- **Head is in the clouds**

  Meaning: If a person has their head in the clouds, they have unrealistic, impractical ideas.
- **Head is mince**

  Meaning: When someone's thoughts are in a state of abject confusion, especially when facing a severe dilemma, their head is mince.
- **Head nor tail**

  Meaning: If you can't make head nor tail of something, you cannot understand it at all or make any sense of it.
- **Head on a spike**

  Meaning: If someone wants a head on a spike, they want to be able to destroy or really punish a person.
- **Head over heels in love**

  Meaning: When someone falls passionately in love and is intoxicated by the feeling has fallen head over heels in love.
- **Head south**

  Meaning: If something head south, it begins to fail or start going bad. 'The project proceeded well for the first two months, but then it headed south.'
- **Heads will roll**

  Meaning: If heads will roll, people will be punished or sacked for something that has gone wrong.

- **Healthy as a horse**
  Meaning: If you're as healthy as a horse, you're very healthy.
- **Hear a pin drop**
  Meaning: If there is complete silence in a room, you can hear a pin drop.
- **Hear on the grapevine**
  Meaning: To receive information indirectly through a series of third parties, similar to a rumour.
- **Heart in the right place**
  Meaning: If someone's heart is in the right place, they are good and kind, though they might not always appear to be so.
- **Heart in your boots**
  Meaning: If you're heart is in your boots, you are very unhappy.
- **Heart in your mouth**
  Meaning: If your heart is in your mouth, then you feel nervous or scared.
- **Heart isn't in it**
  Meaning: If your heart is not in something, then you don't really believe in it or support it.
- **Heart misses a beat**
  Meaning: If your heart misses a beat, you are suddenly shocked or surprised.
- **Heart of glass**
  Meaning: When someone has a heart of glass, they are easily affected emotionally.
- **Heart of gold**
  Meaning: Someone with a heart of gold is a genuinely kind and caring person.
- **Heart of steel**
  Meaning: When someone has a heart of steel, they do not show emotion or are not affected emotionally.
- **Heart-to-heart**
  Meaning: A heart-to-heart is a frank and honest conversation

with someone, where you talk honestly and plainly about issues, no matter how painful.

- **Heaven only knows**

  Meaning: The answer to a question is not or cannot be known. For example, heaven only knows when the war will end.
- **Heavy-handed**

  Meaning: If someone is heavy-handed, they are insensitive and use excessive force or authority when dealing with a problem.
- **Hedge your bets**

  Meaning: If you hedge your bets, you don't risk everything on one opportunity, but try more than one thing.
- **Hell for leather**

  Meaning: If you do something hell for leather, especially running, you do it as fast as you can.
- **Hell in a handcart**

  Meaning: If something is going to hell in a handcart, it is getting worse and worse, with no hope of stopping the decline.
- **Herding cats**

  Meaning: If you have to try to co-ordinate a very difficult situation, where people want to do very different things, you are herding cats.
- **Here today, gone tomorrow**

  Meaning: Money, happiness and other desirable things are often here today, gone tomorrow, which means that they don't last for very long.
- **Hide nor hair**

  Meaning: When there's no trace of something or a person, you haven't seen hide nor hair of it or them.
- **Hiding to nothing**

  Meaning: If people are on a hiding to nothing, their schemes and plans have no chance of succeeding.
- **High and dry**

  Meaning: If you are left high and dry, you are left alone and given no help at all when you need it.

- **High and low**
  Meaning: If you search high and low, you look everywhere for something or someone.
- **High and mighty**
  Meaning: The high and mighty are the people with authority and power. If a person is high and mighty, they behave in a superior and condescending way.
- **High as a kite**
  Meaning: If someone's as high as a kite, it means they have had too much to drink or are under the influence of drugs.
- **High on the hog**
  Meaning: To live in great comfort with lots of money.
- **High-handed**
  Meaning: If someone is high-handed, they behave arrogantly and pompously.
- **High-wire act**
  Meaning: A high-wire act is a dangerous or risky strategy, plan, task, etc.
- **Highway robbery**
  Meaning: Something that is ridiculously expensive, especially when you have no choice but to pay, is a highway robbery.
- **Himalayan blunder**
  Meaning: A Himalayan blunder is a very serious mistake or error.
- **Hindsight is twenty-twenty**
  Meaning: After something has gone wrong, it is easy to look back and make criticisms.
- **His stick doesn't make noise.**
  Meaning: God's justice is always done.
- **Hit a nerve**
  Meaning: If something hits a nerve, it upsets someone or causes them pain, often when it is something they are trying to hide.
- **Hit and miss**
  Meaning: Something that is hit and miss is unpredictable and may produce results or may fail.

- **Hit rock bottom**

  Meaning: When someone hits rock bottom, they reach a point in life where things could not get any worse.

- **Hit rough weather**

  Meaning: If you hit rough weather, you experience difficulties or problems.

- **Hit the airwaves**

  Meaning: If someone hits the airwaves, they go on radio and TV to promote something or to tell their side of a story.

- **Hit the ceiling**

  Meaning: If someone hits the ceiling, they lose their temper and become very angry.

- **Hit the Dirt**

  Meaning: To duck out of the way or fall to the ground to avoid something dangerous.

- **Hit the fan**

  Meaning: When it hits the fan, or, more rudely, the shit hits the fan, serious trouble starts.

- **Hit the ground running**

  Meaning: If someone hits the ground running, they start a new job or position in a very dynamic manner.

- **Hit the mark**

  Meaning: If someone hits the mark, they are right about something.

- **Hit the nail on the head**

  Meaning: If someone hits the nail on the head, they are exactly right about something.

- **Hit the right note**

  Meaning: If you hit the right note, you speak or act in a way that has a positive effect on people.

- **Hit the road**

  Meaning: When people hit the road, they leave a place to go somewhere else.

- **Hit the roof**

  Meaning: If you lose your temper and get very angry, you hit the roof.

- **Hit the sack**

  Meaning: When you hit the sack, you go to bed.

- **Hobson's choice**

  Meaning: A Hobson's choice is something that appears to be a free choice, but is really no choice as there is no genuine alternative.

- **Hoist with your own petard**

  Meaning: If you are hoist with your own petard, you get into trouble or caught in a trap that you had set for someone else.

- **Hold all the aces**

  Meaning: If you hold all the aces, you have all the advantages and your opponents or rivals are in a weak position.

- **Hold the baby**

  Meaning: If someone is responsible for something, they are holding the baby.

- **Hold the bag**

  Meaning: If someone is responsible for something, they are holding the bag.

- **Hold the fort**

  Meaning: If you hold the fort, you look after something or assume someone's responsibilities while they are away.

- **Hold the torch**

  Meaning: If you hold the torch for someone, you have an unrequited or unspoken love.

- **Hold your horses**

  Meaning: If someone tells you to hold your horses, you are doing something too fast and they would like you to slow down.

- **Hold your tongue**

  Meaning: If you hold your tongue, you keep silent even though you want to speak.

- **Holier-than-thou**

  Meaning: Someone who is holier-than-thou believes that they are morally superior to other people.
- **Hollow leg**

  Meaning: Someone who has a hollow leg eats what seems to be more than his stomach can hold.
- **Hollow lentil makes more noise**

  Meaning: Those who are not capable of delivering talk more.
- **Hollow victory**

  Meaning: A hollow victory is where someone wins something in name, but are seen not to have gained anything by winning.
- **Holy smoke!**

  Meaning: This is a way of expressing surprise.
- **Home and hearth**

  Meaning: 'Home and hearth' is an idiom evoking warmth and security.
- **Home stretch**

  Meaning: The home stretch is the last part of something, like a journey, race or project.
- **Home sweet home**

  Meaning: This is said when one is pleased to be back at one's own home.
- **Honours are even**

  Meaning: If honours are even, then a competition has ended with neither side emerging as a winner.
- **Hook, line, and sinker**

  Meaning: If somebody accepts or believes something hook, line, and sinker, they accept it completely.
- **Hooked**

  Meaning: You're hooked when you're obsessed with or addicted to something.
- **Hop, skip, and a jump**

  Meaning: If a place is a hop, skip, and a jump from somewhere, it's only a short distance away.

- **Hope against hope**

  Meaning: If you hope against hope, you hope for something even though there is little or no chance of your wish being fulfilled.

- **Hope in hell**

  Meaning: If something hasn't got a hope in hell, it stands absolutely no chance of succeeding.

- **Hornets' nest**

  Meaning: A hornets' nest is a violent situation or one with a lot of dispute.

- **Horse of a different colour**

  Meaning: If something is a horse of a different colour, it's a different matter or separate issue altogether.

- **Horses for courses**

  Meaning: Horses for courses means that what is suitable for one person or situation might be unsuitable for another.

- **Hostile takeover**

  Meaning: If a company is bought out when it does not want to be, it is known as a hostile takeover.

- **Hot air**

  Meaning: Language that is full of words but means little or nothing is hot air.

- **Hot as blue blazes**

  Meaning: If something's as hot as blue blazes, it's extremely hot.

- **Hot as Hades**

  Meaning: If something's as hot as Hades, it's extremely hot.

- **Hot button**

  Meaning: A hot button is a topic or issue that people feel very strongly about.

- **Hot foot**

  Meaning: If you hot foot it out of a place, you leave very quickly, often running.

- **Hot potato**

  Meaning: A problem or issue that is very controversial and no one wants to deal with is a hot potato.
- **Hot ticket**

  Meaning: A hot ticket is something that is very much in demand at the moment.
- **Hot to trot**

  Meaning: If someone is hot to trot, they are sexually aroused or eager to do something.
- **Hot under the collar**

  Meaning: If you're hot under the collar, you're feeling angry or bothered.
- **Hot water**

  Meaning: If you get into hot water, you get into trouble.
- **Hot-blooded**

  Meaning: Someone who is hot-blooded is easily excitable or passionate.
- **Hot-headed**

  Meaning: A hot-headed person gets angry very easily.
- **Hour of need**

  Meaning: A time when someone really needs something, almost a last chance, is their hour of need.
- **House of cards**

  Meaning: Something that is poorly thought out and can easily collapse or fail is a house of cards.
- **How's tricks?**

  Meaning: This is used as a way of asking people how they are and how things have been going in their life.
- **Humming and harring**

  Meaning: If someone is humming and harring, they are unsure about a decision and can't make their mind up.
- **Hundred blows of goldsmith is comparable to one blow of ironsmith**

  Meaning: One powerful blow is comparable to a hundred smaller blows.

- **Hungry as a bear**

  Meaning: If you are hungry as a bear, it means that you are really hungry.
- **Hunky Dory**

  Meaning: If something is hunky dory, it is perfectly satisfactory, fine.
- **Hush-hush**

  Meaning: If something is hush-hush it is confidential.

I

- **I'll be a monkey's uncle**

  Meaning: Expression of surprise.
- **I'll cross that road when I come to it**

  Meaning: I'll think about something just when it happens, not in advance.
- **I'll eat my hat**

  Meaning: You can say this when you are absolutely sure that you are right to let the other person know that there is no chance of your being wrong.
- **I've got a bone to pick with you**

  Meaning: If somebody says this, they mean that they have some complaint to make against the person they are addressing.
- **Icing on the cake**

  Meaning: This expression is used to refer to something good that happens on top of an already good thing or situation.
- **Idle hands are the devil's handiwork**

  Meaning: When someone is not busy, or being productive, trouble is bound to follow.
- **If at first you don't succeed try again**

  Meaning: When you fail, try until you get it right!
- **If the end is good then all is good**

  Meaning: All's well that ends well.
- **If it ain't broke, don't fix it**

  Meaning: Any attempt to improve on a system that already works is pointless and may even hurt it.

- **If the shoe fits, wear it**

  Meaning: This is used to suggest that something that has been said might apply to a person.

- **If you are given lemons make lemonade**

  Meaning: Always try and make the best out of a bad situation.

- **If you lie down with dogs, you will get up with fleas**

  Meaning: This means that if you become involved with bad company, there will be negative consequences.

- **If you'll pardon my French**

  Meaning: This idiom is used as a way of apologising for swearing.

- **Ill at ease**

  Meaning: If someone is ill at ease, they are worried or uncomfortable.

- **Ill-gotten gains**

  Meaning: Ill-gotten gains are profits or benefits that are made either illegally or unfairly.

- **In a cleft stick**

  Meaning: If you are in a cleft stick, you are in a difficult situation, caught between choices.

- **In a dog's age**

  Meaning: I you haven't done something in a dog's age, you haven't done it for a very long time.

- **In a fix**

  Meaning: If you are in a fix, you are in trouble.

- **In a flash**

  Meaning: If something happens in a flash, it happens very quickly indeed.

- **In a fog**

  Meaning: If you're in a fog, you are confused, dazed or unaware.

- **In a heartbeat**

  Meaning: If something happens very quickly or immediately, it happens in a heartbeat.

- **In a jam**

  Meaning: If you are in a jam, you are in some trouble. If you get out of a jam, you avoid trouble.

- **In a jiffy**

  Meaning: If something happens in a jiffy, it happens very quickly.

- **In a nutshell**

  Meaning: This idiom is used to introduce a concise summary.

- **In a pickle**

  Meaning: If you are in a pickle, you are in some trouble or a mess.

- **In a rut**

  Meaning: In a settled or established pattern, habit or course of action, especially a boring one.

- **In a tick**

  Meaning: If someone will do something in a tick, they'll do it very soon or very quickly.

- **In a tight spot**

  Meaning: If you're in a tight spot, you're in a difficult situation.

- **In an instant**

  Meaning: If something happens in an instant, it happens very rapidly.

- **In apple-pie order**

  Meaning: If something is in apple-pie order, it is very neat and organized.

- **In broad daylight**

  Meaning: If a crime or problem happens in broad daylight, it happens during the day and should have been seen and stopped.

- **In cahoots**

  Meaning: If people are in cahoots, they are conspiring together.

- **In cold blood**

  Meaning: If something is done in cold blood, it is done ruthlessly, without any emotion.

- **In dire straits**

  Meaning: If you're in dire straits, you're in serious trouble or difficulties.
- **In donkey's years**

  Meaning: A very long time.
- **In dribs and drabs**

  Meaning: If people arrive in dribs and drabs, they come in small groups at irregular intervals.
- **In droves**

  Meaning: When things happen in droves, a lot happen at the same time or very quickly.
- **In embryo**

  Meaning: If something is in embryo, it exists but has not developed.
- **In high gear**

  Meaning: If something is in high gear, it is in a quick-paced mode. If someone is in high gear, they are feverishly on the fast track.
- **In high spirits**

  Meaning: If someone is in high spirits, they are in a very good mood or feeling confident about something.
- **In his cups**

  Meaning: If someone is in their cups, they are drunk.
- **In hot water**

  Meaning: If you are in hot water, you are in serious trouble.
- **In light of**

  Meaning: 'In light of' is similar to 'due to'.
- **In my book**

  Meaning: This idiom means 'in my opinion'.
- **In my good books**

  Meaning: If someone is in your good books, you are pleased with or think highly of them at the moment.
- **In no uncertain terms**

  Meaning: Clearly; precisely; emphatically without doubt.

- **In over your head**

  Meaning: If someone is in over their head, they are out of the depth in something they are involved in, and may end up in a mess.

- **In perfect form**

  Meaning: When something is as it ought to be. Or, when used cynically, it may refer to someone whose excesses are on display; a caricature.

- **In rude health**

  Meaning: If someone's in rude health, they are very healthy and look it.

- **In someone's pocket**

  Meaning: If a person is in someone's pocket, they are dependent, especially financially, on them.

- **In spades**

  Meaning: If you have something in spades, you have a lot of it.

- **In stitches**

  Meaning: If someone is in stitches, they are laughing uncontrollably.

- **In tandem**

  Meaning: If people do things in tandem, they do them at the same time.

- **In that vein**

  Meaning: If you do something in that (or this) vein, you do it in the same distinctive manner or style.

- **In the afterglow**

  Meaning: When people feel joy and happiness following a positive event, they are in the afterglow of it.

- **In the bag**

  Meaning: If something is in the bag, it is certain that you will get it or achieve it

- **In the ballpark**

  Meaning: This means that something is close to the adequate or required value.

- **In the black**

  Meaning: If your bank account is in credit, it is in the black.
- **In the cards**

  Meaning: If something is in the cards, it is bound to occur, it is going to happen, or it is inevitable.
- **In the catbird seat**

  Meaning: If someone is in the catbird seat, they are in an advantageous or superior position.
- **In the clear**

  Meaning: If someone is in the clear, they are no longer suspected of or charged with wrongdoing.
- **In the clink**

  Meaning: If someone is in the clink, they are in prison.
- **In the club**

  Meaning: If a woman's in the club, she's pregnant.
- **In the dark**

  Meaning: If you're in the dark, you don't know what is happening around you.
- **In the dock**

  Meaning: If someone is in the dock, they are on trial in court.
- **In the doghouse**

  Meaning: If someone is in the doghouse, they are in disgrace and very unpopular at the moment.
- **In the driver's seat**

  Meaning: If you are in the driver's seat, you are in charge of something or in control of a situation.
- **In the face of**

  Meaning: If people act in the face of something, they do it despite it or when threatened by it.
- **In the family way**

  Meaning: If a woman is in the family way, she is pregnant.
- **In the flesh**

  Meaning: If you meet or see someone in the flesh you actually meet or see them, rather than seeing them on TV or in other media.

- **In the gravy**

  Meaning: If you're in the gravy, you're rich and make money easily.
- **In the hole**

  Meaning: If someone is in the hole, they have a lot of problems, especially financial ones.
- **In the hot seat**

  Meaning: If someone's in the hot seat, they are the target for a lot of unwelcome criticism and examination.
- **In the know**

  Meaning: If you are in the know, you have access to all the information about something, which other people don't have.
- **In the lap of luxury**

  Meaning: People in the lap of luxury are very wealthy and have everything that money can buy.
- **In the long run**

  Meaning: This means 'over a long period of time', 'in the end' or 'in the final result'.
- **In the loop**

  Meaning: If you're in the loop, you are fully informed about what is happening in a certain area or activity.
- **In the lurch**

  Meaning: If you are left in the lurch, you are suddenly left in an embarrassing or tricky situation.
- **In the making**

  Meaning: When something is in the making, it means it is in the process of being made.
- **In the saddle**

  Meaning: If you're in the saddle, you are in control of a situation.
- **In the same boat**

  Meaning: If people are in the same boat, they are in the same predicament or trouble.

- **In the short run**

  Meaning: This refers to the immediate future.
- **In the soup**

  Meaning: If you're in the soup, you're in trouble.
- **In the swim**

  Meaning: If you are in the swim, you are up-to-date with and fully informed about something.
- **In the swing**

  Meaning: If things are in the swing, they are progressing well.
- **In the twinkling of an eye**

  Meaning: If something happens in the twinkling of an eye, it happens very quickly.
- **In the zone**

  Meaning: If you are in the zone, you are very focused on what you have to do.
- **In turn**

  Meaning: This means one after the other. Example: She spoke to each of the guests in turn.
- **In two minds**

  Meaning: If you are in two minds about something, you can't decide what to do.
- **In your blood**

  Meaning: A trait or liking that is deeply ingrained in someone's personality and unlikely to change is in their blood.
- **In your face**

  Meaning: If someone is in your face, they are direct and confrontational.
- **In your sights**

  Meaning: If you have someone or something in your sights, they are your target to beat.
- **Indian file**

  Meaning: If people walk in Indian file, they walk in a line one behind the other.

- **Indian giver**

  Meaning: An Indian giver gives something, then tries to take it back.

- **Indian summer**

  Meaning: If there is a period of warmer weather in late autumn, it is an Indian summer.

- **Ins and outs**

  Meaning: If you know the ins and outs of something, you know all the details.

- **Inside story**

  Meaning: The inside story is information or an explanation that is known only by people closely involved with something.

- **Into each life some rain must fall**

  Meaning: This means that bad or unfortunate things will happen to everyone at some time.

- **Into thin air**

  Meaning: If something vanishes or disappears without trace, it vanishes into thin air; no-one knows where it has gone.

- **Irons in the fire**

  Meaning: A person who has a few irons in the fire has a number of things working to their advantage at the same time.

- **Is Saul also among the prophets?**

  Meaning: It's a biblical idiom used when somebody known for something bad appears all of a sudden to be doing something very good.

- **It ain't over till the fat lady sings**

  Meaning: This idiom means that until something has officially finished, the result is uncertain.

- **It cost an arm and a leg**

  Meaning: If something costs an arm and a leg, it is very expensive indeed.

- **It cost the earth**

  Meaning: If something costs the earth, it is very expensive indeed.

- **It never rains but it pours**

  Meaning: 'It never rains but it pours' means that when things go wrong, they go very wrong.

- **It takes a village to raise a child**

  Meaning: It takes many people to teach a child all that he or she should know.

- **It takes two to tango**

  Meaning: This idiom is used to suggest that when things go wrong, both sides are involved and neither side is completely innocent.

- **It's an ill wind that blows no good**

  Meaning: This is said when things have gone wrong; the idea being that when bad things happen, there can also be some positive results.

- **It's as broad as it is long**

  Meaning: Used to express that it is impossible to decide between two options because they're equal.

- **It's no use crying over spilt milk**

  Meaning: This idiom means that getting upset after something has gone wrong is pointless; it can't be changed so it should be accepted.

- **Itch to**

  Meaning: If you are itching to do something, you are very eager to do it.

- **Itchy feet**

  Meaning: One gets itchy feet when one has been in one place for a time and wants to travel.

- **Ivory tower**

  Meaning: People who live in ivory towers are detached from the world around them.

J

- **Jack Frost**

  Meaning: If everything has frozen in winter, then Jack Frost has visited.

- **Jack the Lad**

  Meaning: A confident and not very serious young man who behaves as he wants.

- **Jack-of-all-trades**

  Meaning: A jack-of-all-trades is someone that can do many different jobs.

- **Jam on your face**

  Meaning: If you say that someone has jam on their face, they appear to be caught, embarrassed or found guilty.

- **Jam tomorrow**

  Meaning: This idiom is used when people promise good things for the future that will never come.

- **Jersey justice**

  Meaning: Jersey justice is very severe justice.

- **Jet set**

  Meaning: Very wealthy people who travel around the world to attend parties or functions are the jet set.

- **Jet-black**

  Meaning: To emphasise just how black something is, such as someone's hair, we can call it jet-black.

- **Job's comforter**

  Meaning: Someone who says they want to comfort, but actually discomforts people is a Job's comforter.

- **Jobs for the boys**

  Meaning: Where people give jobs, contracts, etc., to their friends and associates, these are jobs for the boys.

- **Jockey for position**

  Meaning: If a number of people want the same opportunity and are struggling to emerge as the most likely candidate, they are jockeying for position.

- **Jog my memory**

  Meaning: If you jog someone's memory, you say words that will help someone trying to remember a thought, event, word, phrase, experience, etc.

- **Johnny on the spot**

  Meaning: A person who is always available; ready, willing, and able to do what needs to be done.
- **Johnny-come-lately**

  Meaning: A Johnny-come-lately is someone who has recently joined something or arrived somewhere, especially when they want to make changes that are not welcome.
- **Joined at the hip**

  Meaning: If people are joined at the hip, they are very closely connected and think the same way.
- **Juggle frogs**

  Meaning: If you are juggling frogs, you are trying to do something very difficult.
- **Jump down someone's throat**

  Meaning: If you jump down someone's throat, you criticise or chastise them severely.
- **Jump on the bandwagon**

  Meaning: If people jump on the bandwagon, they get involved in something that has recently become very popular.
- **Jump the gun**

  Meaning: If you jump the gun, you start doing something before the appropriate time.
- **Jump the track**

  Meaning: Jumping the track is suddenly changing from one plan, activity, idea, etc., to another.
- **Jump through hoops**

  Meaning: If you are prepared to jump through hoops for someone, you are prepared to make great efforts and sacrifices for them.
- **Jump to a conclusion**

  Meaning: If someone jumps to a conclusion, they evaluate or judge something without a sufficient examination of the facts.

- **Jumping Judas!**
  Meaning: An expression of surprise or shock.
- **Jungle out there**
  Meaning: If someone says that it is a jungle out there, they mean that the situation is dangerous and there are no rules.
- **Jury's out**
  Meaning: If the jury's out on an issue, then there is no general agreement or consensus on it.
- **Just around the corner**
  Meaning: If something is just around the corner, then it is expected to happen very soon.
- **Just deserts**
  Meaning: If a bad or evil person gets their just deserts, they get the punishment or suffer the misfortune that it is felt they deserve.
- **Just for the heck of it**
  Meaning: When someone does something just for the heck of it, they do it without a good reason.
- **Just in the nick of time**
  Meaning: If you do something in the nick of time, you just manage to do it just in time, with seconds to spare.
- **Just off the boat**
  Meaning: If someone is just off the boat, they are naive and inexperienced.
- **Just what the doctor ordered**
  Meaning: If something's just what the doctor ordered, it is precisely what is needed.
- **Justice is blind**
  Meaning: Justice is blind means that justice is impartial and objective.

K

- **Kangaroo court**
  Meaning: When people take the law into their own hands and

form courts that are not legal, these are known as kangaroo court.

- **Keen as mustard**

  Meaning: If someone is very enthusiastic, they are as keen as mustard.

- **Keep abreast**

  Meaning: If you keep abreast of things, you stay informed about developments.

- **Keep at bay**

  Meaning: If you keep someone or something at bay, you maintain a safe distance from them.

- **Keep body and soul together**

  Meaning: If you earn enough to cover your basic expenses, but nothing more than that, you earn enough to keep body and soul together.

- **Keep it under your hat**

  Meaning: If you keep something under your hat, you keep it secret.

- **Keep mum**

  Meaning: If you keep mum about something, you keep quiet and don't tell anyone.

- **Keep posted**

  Meaning: If you keep posted about something, you keep up-to-date with information and developments.

- **Keep someone at arm's length**

  Meaning: If you keep someone or something at arm's length, you keep a safe distance away from them.

- **Keep someone on their toes**

  Meaning: If you keep someone on their toes, you make sure that they concentrate on what they are supposed to do.

- **Keep tabs on someone**

  Meaning: If you keep tabs on someone, you check, watch and keep a close eye on what they are doing.

- **Keep the wolf at bay**

  Meaning: If you keep the wolf at bay, you make enough money to avoid going hungry or falling heavily into debt.

- **Keep the wolf from the door**

  Meaning: If you keep the wolf from the door, you have enough money for food and the basic essentials.

- **Keep your eye on the prize**

  Meaning: This means that you should keep your focus on achieving a positive end result.

- **Keep your eyes peeled**

  Meaning: If you keep your eyes peeled, you stay alert or watchful.

- **Keep your fingers crossed**

  Meaning: If you are keeping your fingers crossed, you are hoping for a positive outcome.

- **Keep your hair on**

  Meaning: Keep your hair on is advice telling someone to keep calm and not to over-react or get angry.

- **Keep your head**

  Meaning: If you keep your head, you stay calm in times of difficulty.

- **Keep your head above water**

  Meaning: If you are just managing to survive financially, you are keeping your head above water.

- **Keep your nose to the grindstone**

  Meaning: If you keep your nose to the grindstone, you work hard and seriously.

- **Keep your options open**

  Meaning: If someone's keeping their options open, they aren't going to restrict themselves or rule out any possible course of action.

- **Keep your pants on**

  Meaning: If someone tells you to keep your pants on, they mean that you should be patient and not make them rush.

- **Keep your powder dry**

  Meaning: If you keep your powder dry, you act cautiously so as not to damage your chances.
- **Keep your shirt on!**

  Meaning: This idiom is used to tell someone to calm down.
- **Keep your wig on!**

  Meaning: This idiom is used to tell someone to calm down.
- **Kettle of fish**

  Meaning: A pretty or fine kettle of fish is a difficult problem or situation.
- **Kick a habit**

  Meaning: If you kick a habit, you stop doing it.
- **Kick away the ladder**

  Meaning: If someone kicks away the ladder, they remove something that was supporting or helping someone.
- **Kick in the teeth**

  Meaning: Bad news or a sudden disappointment are a kick in the teeth.
- **Kick something into the long grass**

  Meaning: If an issue or problem is kicked into the long grass, it is pushed aside and hidden in the hope that it will be forgotten or ignored.
- **Kick the bucket**

  Meaning: When someone kicks the bucket, they die.
- **Kick up your heels**

  Meaning: If you kick up your heels, you go to parties or celebrate something.
- **Kick your heels**

  Meaning: If you have to kick your heels, you are forced to wait for the result or outcome of something.
- **Kid gloves**

  Meaning: If someone is handled with kid gloves, they are given special treatment and handled with great care.

- **Kill the fatted calf**

  Meaning: If you kill the fatted calf, you have a celebration, usually to welcome someone who's been away a long time.
- **Kindred spirit**

  Meaning: A kindred spirit is someone who feels and thinks the way you do.
- **King of the castle**

  Meaning: The king of the castle is the person who is in charge of something or in a very comfortable position compared to their companions.
- **King's ransom**

  Meaning: If something costs or is worth a king's ransom, it costs or is worth a lot of money.
- **Kiss of death**

  Meaning: The kiss of death is an action that means failure or ruin for someone, a scheme, a plan, etc.
- **Kiss something goodbye**

  Meaning: If someone tells you that you can kiss something goodbye, you have no chance of getting or having it.
- **Kissing cousin**

  Meaning: A kissing cousin is someone you are related to, but not closely.
- **Kitchen-sink**

  Meaning: Kitchen-sink drama deals with ordinary people's lives.
- **Knee slapper**

  Meaning: A knee slapper is something that is considered funny, though it is often used sarcastically.
- **Knee-jerk reaction**

  Meaning: A knee-jerk reaction is an instant, instinctive response to a situation.
- **Knight in shining armour**

  Meaning: A knight in shining armour is someone who saves you when you are in great trouble or danger.

- **Knit your brows**

  Meaning: If you knit your brows, you frown or look worried.
- **Knock on wood**

  Meaning: This idiom is used to wish for good luck.
- **Knock something on the head**

  Meaning: If you knock something on the head, you stop it or stop doing it.
- **Knock the pins from under someone**

  Meaning: If someone knocks the pins from under you, they let you down.
- **Knock your block off**

  Meaning: To punch someone in the face.
- **Knock your socks off**

  Meaning: If something knocks your socks off, it amazes and surprises you, usually in a positive way.
- **Know a hawk from a handsaw**

  Meaning: If someone knows a hawk from a handsaw, they are able to distinguish things and assess them.
- **Know full well**

  Meaning: When you know full well, you are absolutely sure that you know.
- **Know the ropes**

  Meaning: Someone who is experienced and knows how the system works know the ropes.
- **Know which side one's bread is buttered on**

  Meaning: If you know which side one's bread is buttered on, you know where your interests lie and will act accordingly to protect or further them.
- **Know which way the wind blows**

  Meaning: This means that you should know how things are developing and be prepared for the future.
- **Know your onions**

  Meaning: If someone is very well-informed about something, they know their onions.

- **Know your place**

  Meaning: A person who knows their place doesn't try to impose themselves on others.

L

- **Labour of love**

  Meaning: A labour of love is a project or task undertaking for the interest or pleasure in doing it rather than the reward, financial or otherwise.
- **Lame duck**

  Meaning: If something or someone is a lame duck, they are in trouble.
- **Land of nod**

  Meaning: If someone has gone to the land of nod, they have fallen asleep or gone to bed.
- **Landslide victory**

  Meaning: A landslide victory is a victory in an election by a very large margin.
- **Lap dog**

  Meaning: A lap dog is a person who is eager to please another at the expense of his or her own needs in order to maintain a position of privilege or favour.
- **Lap of the gods**

  Meaning: If something is in the lap of the gods, it is beyond our control and fate will decide the outcome.
- **Larger than life**

  Meaning: If something is excessive or exaggerated, it is larger than life.
- **Last hurrah**

  Meaning: If an elderly person does something special before they die, it is a last hurrah.
- **Last laugh**

  Meaning: The person who has the last laugh ends up with the the advantage in a situation after some setbacks.

- **Last-ditch**

  Meaning: A last-ditch attempt is a desperate attempt that will probably fail anyway.

- **Late bloomer**

  Meaning: When someone does not obtain success with their interests, talents, or personality until later in their lives, we say they are a late bloomer.

- **Laugh a minute**

  Meaning: Someone who is a laugh a minute is very funny.

- **Laugh to see a pudding crawl**

  Meaning: Someone who would laugh to see a pudding crawl is easily amused and will laugh at anything.

- **Laugh up your sleeve**

  Meaning: If you laugh up your sleeve, you laugh at someone secretly.

- **Laughter is the best medicine**

  Meaning: Laughing is often helpful for healing, especially emotional healing.

- **Law unto yourself**

  Meaning: If somebody's a law unto themselves, they do what they believe is right regardless of what is generally accepted as correct.

- **Lay down the law**

  Meaning: If someone lays down the law, they tell people what to do and are authoritarian.

- **Lay it on thick**

  Meaning: If someone lays it on thick, they make an emotion or experience seem more important or serious than it really is.

- **Lay of the land**

  Meaning: The lay of the land is the way something is organized, runs, is arranged, etc.

- **Lay waste**

  Meaning: To lay waste to something is to destroy it.

- **Lead with the chin**

  Meaning: If someone leads with their chin, they speak or behave without fear of the consequences.

- **Lean and mean**

  Meaning: An organization that is lean and mean has no excess or unnecessary elements and is very competitive.

- **Learn the ropes**

  Meaning: If you are learning the ropes, you are learning how to do something.

- **Leave no stone unturned**

  Meaning: If you look everywhere to find something, or try everything to achieve something, you leave no stone unturned.

- **Leave well alone**

  Meaning: If you leave something well alone, you keep a safe distance from it, either physically or metaphorically.

- **Left in the dark**

  Meaning: If you are left in the dark about something, you aren't given the information that you should have.

- **Left to your own devices**

  Meaning: If someone is left to their own devices, they are not controlled and can do what they want.

- **Left-handed compliment**

  Meaning: A left-handed compliment is one that sounds like praise but has an insulting meaning.

- **Lend an ear**

  Meaning: If you lend an ear, you listen to what someone has to say.

- **Leopard can't change its spots**

  Meaning: This idiom means that people cannot change basic aspects of their character, especially negative ones.

- **Lesser of two evils**

  Meaning: Something that is the lesser of two evils, is an unpleasant option, but not as bad as the other.

- **Let sleeping dogs lie**

  Meaning: If someone is told to let sleeping dogs lie, it means that they shouldn't disturb a situation as it would result in trouble or complications.
- **Let the genie out of the bottle**

  Meaning: If people let the genie out of the bottle, they let something bad happen that cannot be put right or controlled.
- **Let the grass grow round your feet**

  Meaning: If you let the grass grow round your feet, you delay doing things instead of taking action.
- **Let your guard down**

  Meaning: If you let your guard down, you relax and stop looking out for danger.
- **Let your hair down**

  Meaning: If someone lets their hair down, they relax and stop feeling inhibited or shy.
- **Let's call it a day**

  Meaning: This is used as a way of suggesting that it is time to stop working on something.
- **Letter of the law**

  Meaning: If people interpret laws and regulations strictly, ignoring the ideas behind them, they follow the letter of the law.
- **Level best**

  Meaning: If you do your level best, you make every possible effort to do something as well as you can.
- **Level playing field**

  Meaning: If there's a level playing field everybody is treated equally.
- **License to print money**

  Meaning: A license to print money is something that generates a large income without much effort.
- **Lie low**

  Meaning: If someone lies low, they try not to be found or caught.

- **Lie through your teeth**

  Meaning: Someone who is always lying, regardless of what people know, lies through their teeth.
- **Life and limb**

  Meaning: When people risk life and limb, they could be killed or suffer serious injuries.
- **Life is just a bowl of cherries**

  Meaning: This idiom means that life is simple and pleasant.
- **Light a fire under**

  Meaning: If you light a fire under somebody, you strongly motivate them to work faster.
- **Light bulb moment**

  Meaning: A light bulb moment is when you have a sudden realisation about something, like the light bulbs used to indicate an idea in cartoons.
- **Light on your feet**

  Meaning: If someone is light on their feet, they can move quickly and are agile.
- **Light years ahead**

  Meaning: If you are light years ahead of others, you are a long way in front of them in terms of development, success, etc.
- **Lightning rod**

  Meaning: Someone or something that attracts a lot of negative comment, often diverting attention from other problems, is a lightning rod.
- **Like a bat out of hell**

  Meaning: This expression means extremely quickly.
- **Like a bear with a sore head**

  Meaning: If someone's like a bear with a sore head, they complain a lot and are unhappy about something.
- **Like a bull at a gate**

  Meaning: If you tackle a job very quickly, without any real thought about what you are doing, you are going at it like a bull at a gate.

- **Like a cat on hot bricks**

  Meaning: If someone is like a cat on hot bricks, they are very nervous or excited.

- **Like a cat that got the cream**

  Meaning: If someone looks very pleased with themselves and happy, they look like a cat that got the cream.

- **Like a duck to water**

  Meaning: If someone has a natural talent for something and enjoys it, they take to it like a duck to water.

- **Like a fish out of water**

  Meaning: If someone feels like a fish out of water, they are very uncomfortable in the situation they are in.

- **Like a hawk**

  Meaning: If you watch something or someone like a hawk, you observe very closely and carefully.

- **Like a headless chicken**

  Meaning: If someone rushes about like a headless chicken, they move very fast all over the place, usually without thinking.

- **Like a kid in a candy store**

  Meaning: If someone is like a kid in a candy store, they are very excited about something.

- **Like a moth to a flame**

  Meaning: Something that is like a moth to a flame is attracted to something that is deadly or dangerous.

- **Like Chinese arithmetic**

  Meaning: If something is complicated and hard to understand, it's like Chinese arithmetic.

- **Like clockwork**

  Meaning: If something happens like clockwork, it happens at very regular times or intervals.

- **Like father, like son**

  Meaning: This idiom is used when different generations of a family behave in the same way or have the same talents of defects.

- **Like giving a donkey strawberries**

  Meaning: If something is like giving a donkey strawberries, people fail to appreciate its value.

- **Like green corn through the new maid**

  Meaning: If something is very fast, it is like green corn through the new maid.

- **Like lambs to the slaughter**

  Meaning: If somebody does something unpleasant without any resistance, they go like lambs to the slaughter.

- **Like peas in a pod**

  Meaning: If people or things are like peas in a pod, they look identical.

- **Like pulling teeth**

  Meaning: If something if like pulling teeth, it is very difficult, especially if trying to extract information or to get a straight answer from someone.

- **Like there's no tomorrow**

  Meaning: If you do something like there's no tomorrow, you do it fast or energetically.

- **Like two peas in a pod**

  Meaning: Things that are like two peas in a pod are very similar or identical.

- **Lion's share**

  Meaning: The lion's share of something is the biggest or best part.

- **Live and let live**

  Meaning: If you live and let live, you accept other people as they are, although they may have a different way of life.

- **Live high off the hog**

  Meaning: If you are living high off the hog, you are living lavishly.

- **Live wire**

  Meaning: A person who is very active, both mentally and physically, is a live wire.

- **Lo and behold**

  Meaning: This phrase is used to express surprise.
- **Loan shark**

  Meaning: A loan shark lends money at very high rates of interest.
- **Lock and load**

  Meaning: This is a military term meaning "be ready and prepared".
- **Lock horns**

  Meaning: When people lock horns, they argue or fight about something.
- **Lock the stable door after the horse has bolted**

  Meaning: If someone takes action too late, they do this; there is no reason to lock an empty stable.
- **Lone wolf**

  Meaning: A lone wolf is a person who prefers to do things on their own or without help from other people.
- **Long face**

  Meaning: Someone with a long face is sad or depressed about something.
- **Long in the tooth**

  Meaning: If someone is long in the tooth, they are a bit too old to do something.
- **Long shot**

  Meaning: If something is a long shot, there is only a very small chance of success.
- **Long time no hear**

  Meaning: The speaker could say this when they have not heard from a person, either through phone calls or emails for a long time.
- **Long time no see**

  Meaning: 'Long time no see' means that the speaker has not seen that person for a long time.

- **Look before you leap**

  Meaning: This idiom means that you should think carefully about the possible results or consequences before doing something.

- **Look on the bright side**

  Meaning: If you look on the bright side, you try to see things in an optimistic way, especially when something has gone wrong.

- **Look what the cat dragged in**

  Meaning: This idiom is used when someone arrives somewhere looking a mess or flustered and bothered.

- **Loose end**

  Meaning: A loose end is an unresolved problem or unfinished business.

- **Lord love a duck**

  Meaning: An exclamation used when nothing else will fit. Often fitting when one is stunned or dismayed.

- **Lose face**

  Meaning: To lose one's reputation or standing is to lose face.

- **Lose the plot**

  Meaning: If someone loses the plot, they have stopped being rational about something.

- **Lose your marbles**

  Meaning: If someone has lost their marbles, they've gone mad.

- **Lose your rag**

  Meaning: Is someone loses their rag, they are very angry about something.

- **Lose your shirt**

  Meaning: If someone loses their shirt, they lose all their money through a bad investment, gambling, etc.

- **Love is blind**

  Meaning: If you love someone, it doesn't matter what they look like. You will also overlook faults.

- **Love me, love my dog**

  Meaning: If you love someone, you should accept everything about them and the people they like.

- **Low-hanging fruit**

  Meaning: Low-hanging fruit are things that are easily achieved.
- **Lower the bar**

  Meaning: If people change the standards required to make things easier, they lower the bar.
- **Lower your sights**

  Meaning: If you lower your sights, you accept something that is less than you were hoping for.

M

- **Mad as a badger**

  Meaning: If someone is as mad as a badger, they are crazy.
- **Mad as a cut snake**

  Meaning: One who is mad as a cut snake has lost all sense of reason, is crazy, out of control.
- **Mad as a hornet**

  Meaning: If someone is as mad as a hornet, they are very angry indeed.
- **Mad as a March hare**

  Meaning: Someone who is excitable and unpredictable is as mad as a March hare.
- **Mad as a wet hen**

  Meaning: If someone is as mad as a wet hen, they are extremely angry.
- **Made in the shade**

  Meaning: One has an easy time in life or in a given situation. Finding things working to one's benefit.
- **Made of money**

  Meaning: If you are made of money, you have a lot of money.
- **Major league**

  Meaning: Something major league is very important.

- **Make a better fist**

  Meaning: If someone makes a better fist of doing something, they do a better job.

- **Make a clean breast**

  Meaning: If someone makes a clean breast, they confess in full to something they have done.

- **Make a killing**

  Meaning: If you make a killing, you do something that makes you a lot of money.

- **Make a meal**

  Meaning: If someone makes a meal of something, they spend too long doing it or make it look more difficult than it really is.

- **Make a mint**

  Meaning: If someone is making a mint, they are making a lot of money.

- **Make a monkey of someone**

  Meaning: If you make a monkey of someone, you make them look foolish.

- **Make a mountain out of a molehill**

  Meaning: If somebody makes a mountain out of a molehill, they exaggerate the importance or seriousness of a problem.

- **Make a pig's ear**

  Meaning: If you make a pig's ear of something, you make a mess of it.

- **Make a pitch**

  Meaning: If you make a pitch for something, you make a bid, offer or other attempt to get it.

- **Make a request**

  Meaning: If you request something, or make a request, you are asking for something you want or need.

- **Make a rod for your own back**

  Meaning: If you make a rod for your own back, you make something difficult for yourself.

- **Make a song and dance**

  Meaning: If someone makes a song and dance, they make an unnecessary fuss about something unimportant.

- **Make a virtue out of necessity**

  Meaning: If you make a virtue out of necessity, you make the best of a difficult or unsatisfactory situation.

- **Make an enquiry**

  Meaning: If you make an enquiry, you ask for general information about something.

- **Make it snappy**

  Meaning: To do something quickly: Make it snappy, will you, because I need help right now.

- **Make money hand over fist**

  Meaning: If you make money hand over fist, you make a lot of money without any difficulty.

- **Make my day**

  Meaning: If something makes your day, it satisfies you or makes you happy.

- **Make no bones about it**

  Meaning: If somebody make no bones about a scandal in their past, they are open and honest about it and show no shame or embarrassment.

- **Make or break**

  Meaning: A make or break decision, stage, etc., is a crucial one that will determine the success or failure of the whole venture.

- **Make out like a bandit**

  Meaning: If someone is extremely successful in a venture, they make out like a bandit.

- **Make waves**

  Meaning: If someone makes waves, they cause a lot of trouble.

- **Make you spit**

  Meaning: If something makes you spit, it irritates you or makes you angry.

- **Make your blood boil**
  Meaning: If something makes your blood boil, it makes you very angry.
- **Make your hair stand on end**
  Meaning: If something makes your hair stand on end, it terrifies you.
- **Make your toes curl**
  Meaning: If something makes your toes curl, it makes you feel very uncomfortable, shocked or embarrassed.
- **Make yourself scarce**
  Meaning: If someone makes themselves scarce, they go away from a place, especially to avoid trouble or so that they can't be found.
- **Man in the street**
  Meaning: The man in the street is an idiom to describe ordinary people, especially when talking about their opinions and ideas.
- **Man of his word**
  Meaning: A man of his word is a person who does what he says and keeps his promises.
- **Man of letters**
  Meaning: A man of letters is someone who is an expert in the arts and literature, and often a writer too.
- **Man of means**
  Meaning: A man, or woman, of means is wealthy.
- **Man of parts**
  Meaning: A man of parts is a person who is talented in a number of different areas or ways.
- **Man of straw**
  Meaning: A weak person that can easily be beaten of changed is a man of straw.
- **Man of the cloth**
  Meaning: A man of the cloth is a priest.
- **Man proposes, God disposes**
  Meaning: Your fate lies in the hands of God.

- **Man upstairs**

  Meaning: When people refer to the man upstairs, they are referring to God.

- **Man's man**

  Meaning: A man's man is a man who does things enjoyed by men and is respected by other men.

- **Many a slip twixt cup and lip**

  Meaning: There's many a slip twixt cup and lip means that many things can go wrong before something is achieved.

- **Many hands make light work**

  Meaning: This idiom means that when everyone gets involved in something, the work gets done quickly.

- **Many happy returns**

  Meaning: This expression is used to wish someone a happy birthday.

- **Many moons ago**

  Meaning: A very long time ago.

- **March to the beat of your own drum**

  Meaning: If people march to the beat of their own drum, they do things the way they want without taking other people into consideration.

- **Mark someone's card**

  Meaning: If you mark someone's card, you correct them in a forceful and prompt manner when they say something wrong.

- **Marked man**

  Meaning: A marked man is a person who is being targeted by people who want to do them harm or cause them trouble.

- **Marriage of convenience**

  Meaning: A marriage of convenience is a marriage or commitment made for financial, social or other benefit rather than love, affection, etc.

- **Master of a line**

  Meaning: To go about the same old beaten path.

- **Mealy-mouthed**

  Meaning: A mealy-mouthed person doesn't say what they mean clearly.
- **Meat and drink**

  Meaning: If something is meat and drink to you, you enjoy it and are naturally good at it, though many find it difficult.
- **Meet someone halfway**

  Meaning: If you meet someone halfway, you accept some of their ideas and make concessions.
- **Meet your expectations**

  Meaning: If something doesn't meet your expectations, it means that it wasn't as good as you had thought it was going to be; a disappointment.
- **Meet your Maker**

  Meaning: If someone has gone to meet their Maker, they have died.
- **Meet your match**

  Meaning: If you meet your match, you meet a person who is at least as good if not better than you are at something.
- **Melt your heart**

  Meaning: If something melts your heart, it affects you emotionally and you cannot control the feeling.
- **Melting pot**

  Meaning: A melting pot is a place where people from many ethnicities and nationalities live together.
- **Mess with a bull, you get the horns**

  Meaning: If you do something stupid or dangerous, you can get hurt.
- **Method in his madness**

  Meaning: If there's method in someone's madness, they do things in a strange and unorthodox way, but manage to get results.
- **Mexican standoff**

  Meaning: When there is a deadlock in strategy and neither side can do anything that will ensure victory, it's a Mexican standoff.

- **Mickey Mouse**

  Meaning: If something is Mickey Mouse, it is intellectually trivial or not of a very high standard.

- **Middle of nowhere**

  Meaning: If someone says that he/she is in the middle of nowhere, he/she means that he/she is not sure where he/she is.

- **Mighty oaks from little acorns grow**

  Meaning: Big or great things start very small.

- **Mile a minute**

  Meaning: To do something very quickly. For example: He was talking a mile a minute.

- **Milk run**

  Meaning: A milk run is a short trip, stopping in a number of places.

- **Millstone round your neck**

  Meaning: A millstone around your neck is a problem that prevents you from doing what you want to do.

- **Mince words**

  Meaning: If people mince words, or mince their words, they don't say what they really mean clearly.

- **Mind over matter**

  Meaning: This idiom is used when someone uses their willpower to rise above adversity.

- **Mind your own beeswax**

  Meaning: This idiom means that people should mind their own business and not interfere in other people's affairs.

- **Mind your P's and Q's**

  Meaning: This is used as a way of telling someone to be polite and behave well.

- **Mint condition**

  Meaning: If something is in mint condition, it is in perfect condition.

- **Misery guts**

  Meaning: A misery guts is a person who's always unhappy and tries to make others feel negative.
- **Miss is as good as a mile**

  Meaning: A miss is as good as a mile means that if you fail, even by the smallest margin, it is still a failure.
- **Miss the boat**

  Meaning: If you miss the boat, you are too late to take advantage of an opportunity.
- **Monkey doesn't know the taste of ginger**

  Meaning: Those who don't know, can't appreciate.
- **My heart goes out to someone**

  Meaning: If your heart goes out to someone, you feel genuine sympathy for them.
- **My way or the highway**

  Meaning: This idiom is used to say that if people don't do what you say, they will have to leave or quit the project, etc.

N

- **Nail in the coffin**

  Meaning: A nail in someone or something's coffin is a problem or event that is a clear step towards an inevitable failure.
- **Nature abhors a vacuum**

  Meaning: This idiom is used to express the idea that empty or unfilled spaces are unnatural as they go against the laws of nature and physics.
- **Near the knuckle**

  Meaning: If something is near the knuckle, it is bit explicit or too close to the truth for comfort
- **Neck and neck**

  Meaning: If two competitors or candidates, etc., are neck and neck, then they are very close and neither is clearly winning.

- **Need no introduction**
  Meaning: Someone who is very famous and known to everyone needs no introduction.
- **Neither fish nor fowl**
  Meaning: Something or someone that is neither fish nor fowl doesn't really fit into any one group.
- **Neither here nor there**
  Meaning: If something is neither here nor there, it is of very little importance.
- **Neither is the father nor the brother are big, only money is big.**
  Meaning: Money rules over relationships as well.
- **Neither use nor ornament**
  Meaning: Something that serves no purpose and is not aesthetically pleasing is neither use nor ornament.
- **Nerves of steel**
  Meaning: If someone has nerves of steel, they don't get frightened when other people do.
- **Nervous Nellie**
  Meaning: Someone excessively worried or apprehensive is a nervous Nellie (or Nelly).
- **Nest egg**
  Meaning: If you have some money saved for the future, it is a nest egg.
- **Never a rose without the prick**
  Meaning: This means that good things always have something bad as well; like the thorns on the stem of a rose.
- **Never say die**
  Meaning: One shouldn't give up hope.
- **New blood**
  Meaning: New ideas or people to invigorate something.
- **New kid on the block**
  Meaning: Someone who has recently joined a company,

organization, team, etc., and does not know how things work yet.

- **New lease of life**

  Meaning: If someone finds new enthusiasm and energy for something, they have a new lease of life.

- **New man**

  Meaning: A New man is a man who believes in complete equality of the sexes and shares domestic work equally.

- **New sheriff in town**

  Meaning: This is used when a new authority figure takes charge.

- **New York minute**

  Meaning: If something happens in a New York minute, it happens very fast.

- **Nice as pie**

  Meaning: If a person is nice as pie, they are surprisingly very kind and friendly.

- **Nick of time**

  Meaning: If you do something in the nick of time, you do it at the very last minute or second.

- **Night owl**

  Meaning: A night owl is someone who goes to bed very late.

- **Nine plus two makes eleven**

  Meaning: To run away.

- **Nip and tuck**

  Meaning: A close contest where neither opponent seems to be gaining the advantage.

- **Nip at the bit**

  Meaning: If someone is nipping at the bit, they are anxious to get something done and don't want to wait.

- **Nip it in the bud**

  Meaning: If you nip something in the bud, you deal with a problem when it is still small, before it can grow into something serious.

- **Nitty gritty**

  Meaning: If people get down to the nitty gritty, they concentrate on the most important and serious issues.
- **No bed of roses**

  Meaning: If something isn't a bed of roses, it is difficult.
- **No can do**

  Meaning: No can do means that the speaker can't do whatever it is that has been asked of him or her.
- **No dice**

  Meaning: No dice is a way of refusing to accept or agree to something.
- **No dog in this fight**

  Meaning: If you have no dog in a fight, you are not concerned and will not be affected either way by the outcome of something.
- **No go**

  Meaning: Something that will not work. 'A square peg in a round hole is a no go.'
- **No good deed goes unpunished**

  Meaning: This means that life is unfair and people can do or try to do good things and still end up in a lot of trouble.
- **No great shakes**

  Meaning: If someone is no great shakes at something, they are not very good at it.
- **No holds barred**

  Meaning: If there are no holds barred, there are no rules of conduct; you can do anything.
- **No laughing matter**

  Meaning: Something that is no laughing matter is very serious.
- **No love lost**

  Meaning: If there is no love lost between two people they have a strong enmity towards or hate for the other and make no effort to conceal it.

- **No need for asafoetida or potash alum to get colour**

  Meaning: To have a gain without much effort.
- **No pain, no gain**

  Meaning: Achievements require some sort of sacrifice.
- **No quarter**

  Meaning: This means without mercy. We can say no quarter given or asked.
- **No question**

  Meaning: This idiom means that something is certain or definite.
- **No spine**

  Meaning: If someone has no spine, they lack courage or are cowardly.
- **No spring chicken**

  Meaning: If someone is no spring chicken, they are not young.
- **No strings attached**

  Meaning: If something has no strings attached, there are no obligations or requirements involved.
- **No Sweat**

  Meaning: Something that is easy.
- **No time to lose**

  Meaning: If there's no time to lose, then it's time to get started otherwise it won't be finished on time.
- **No two ways about it**

  Meaning: If there are no two ways about something, there is no other possible interpretation.
- **No use to man or beast**

  Meaning: If something or someone is no use to man or beast, they it or they are utterly useless.
- **Noddy work**

  Meaning: Unimportant or very simple tasks.
- **None so blind as those who will not see**

  Meaning: This idiom is used when people refuse to accept facts presented to them.

- **Nose in the air**

  Meaning: If someone has their nose in the air, they behave in a way that is meant to show that they are superior to others.
- **Nosy parker**

  Meaning: A nosy parker is someone who is excessively interested in other people's lives.
- **Not a snowball's chance in hell**

  Meaning: There is absolutely no possibility of something happening if there's not a snowball's chance in hell.
- **Not all there**

  Meaning: If someone isn't all there, they are a little bit stupid or crazy.
- **Not born yesterday**

  Meaning: When someone says that they weren't born yesterday, they mean that they are not naive or easily fooled.
- **Not cricket**

  Meaning: If something is not cricket, it is unfair.
- **Not enough room to swing a cat**

  Meaning: If a room is very small, you can say that there isn't enough room to swing a cat in it.
- **Not give a monkey's**

  Meaning: If you couldn't give a monkey's about something, you don't care at all about it.
- **Not give the time of day**

  Meaning: If you wouldn't give the time of day to someone, you dislike them so much that you would not even use common courtesy.
- **Not have the heart**

  Meaning: If you don't have the heart to do something, you don't have the strength or courage to do something.
- **Not have two nickels to rub together**

  Meaning: If a person doesn't have two nickels to rub together, they are very poor.

- **Not have two pennies to rub together**

  Meaning: If someone hasn't got two pennies to rub together, they are very poor indeed.
- **Not hurt a fly**

  Meaning: Somebody who would not hurt a fly is not aggressive.
- **Not know beans about**

  Meaning: If someone doesn't know beans about something, they know nothing about it.
- **Not know enough to come in out of the rain**

  Meaning: Someone who doesn't know enough to come in out of the rain is particularly stupid.
- **Not much cop**

  Meaning: Describing a film or something as not much cop is a way of saying that you didn't think much of it.
- **Not my cup of tea**

  Meaning: If something is not your cup of tea, you don't like it very much.
- **Not our bag**

  Meaning: If something is not your bag, it is not really suitable for your needs or you don't like it much.
- **Not the only pebble on the beach**

  Meaning: If something is not the only pebble on the beach, there are other possibilities or alternatives.
- **Not to be sneezed at**

  Meaning: If something is not to be sneezed at, it should be taken seriously.
- **Not wash**

  Meaning: If a story or explanation will not wash, it is not credible.
- **Not worth a red cent**

  Meaning: If something is not worth a red cent, it has no value.
- **Notch on your belt**

  Meaning: A success or achievement that might help you in the future is a notch on your belt.

- **Nothing to crow about**

  Meaning: If something's nothing to crow about, it's not particularly good or special.

- **Nothing to write home about**

  Meaning: Something that is not special or good is nothing to write home about.

- **Nothing ventured, nothing gained**

  Meaning: You can't win if you don't join in the game; if you don't participate in something, you will not achieve anything.

- **Now and then**

  Meaning: This idiom means 'occasionally'.

- **Now I ask you**

  Meaning: Used at the end of a story to express disbelief, or in answer to a question to express a mild indignation.

- **Null and void**

  Meaning: If something's null and void, it is invalid or is no longer applicable.

- **Number cruncher**

  Meaning: A number cruncher is an accountant or someone who is very good at dealing with numbers and calculations.

- **Nuts and bolts**

  Meaning: The nuts and bolts are the most essential components of something.

- **Nutty as a fruitcake**

  Meaning: Someone who's nutty as a fruitcake is irrational or crazy.

O

- **Object lesson**

  Meaning: An object lesson serves as a warning to others.

- **Odds and ends**

  Meaning: Odds and ends are small, remnant articles and things-the same as 'bits and bobs'.

- **Off colour**

  Meaning: If someone looks off colour, they look ill.
- **Off on one**

  Meaning: If someone goes off on one, they get extremely angry indeed.
- **Off the beaten track**

  Meaning: Somewhere that's off the beaten track is in a remote location.
- **Off the chart**

  Meaning: If something goes off the chart, it far exceeds the normal standards, good or bad, for something.
- **Off the cuff**

  Meaning: If you do something off the cuff, you do it without any preparation.
- **Off the grid**

  Meaning: Someone who is off the grid lives outside society and chooses not to follow its rules and conventions.
- **Off the hook**

  Meaning: If someone is off the hook, they have avoided punishment or criticism for something they have done.
- **Off the mark**

  Meaning: If something is off the mark, it is inaccurate or incorrect.
- **Off the rails**

  Meaning: If someone has gone off the rails, they have lost track of reality.
- **Off the scale**

  Meaning: If something goes off the scale, it far exceeds the normal standards, good or bad, for something.
- **Off the shelf**

  Meaning: If a product is off the shelf, it can be used straightaway without any setting-up.
- **Off the top of your head**

  Meaning: If you say something off the top of your head, you don't think about it beforehand.

- **Off the track**

  Meaning: If something puts or throws you off your track, it distracts you or keeps you from achieving what you want.

- **Off your chump**

  Meaning: If someone is off their chump, they are crazy or irrational.

- **Off your rocker**

  Meaning: Someone who is off their rocker is crazy.

- **Oh, my goodness!**

  Meaning: An expression of surprise.

- **Old chestnut**

  Meaning: An old chestnut is something that has been repeated so many times that it has lost its impact.

- **Old flames die hard**

  Meaning: It's very difficult to forget old things, especially the first love.

- **Old friends and old wine are best**

  Meaning: This idiom means that the things and people that we know well are better than the unfamiliar.

- **Old hat**

  Meaning: If something's old hat, it seems rather old fashioned and dated.

- **Old wives' tale**

  Meaning: A proverb or piece of advice that is commonly accepted as truth and is handed down the generations, but is normally false.

- **Older than dirt**

  Meaning: Something or someone's that's older than the dirt is extremely old.

- **Older than the hills**

  Meaning: Something or someone's that's older than the hills is extremely old.

- **Oldest trick in the book**

  Meaning: The oldest trick in the book is a well-known way of deceiving someone, though still effective.

- **Olive branch**

  Meaning: If you hold out or offer an olive branch, you make a gesture to indicate that you want peace.

- **On a silver platter**

  Meaning: If you hand or give something on a silver platter to someone, you let them have it too easily.

- **On all fours**

  Meaning: If someone is on all fours, they crawl.

- **On fire**

  Meaning: If you're on fire, you're doing really well at something.

- **On good terms**

  Meaning: If people are on good terms, they have a good relationship.

- **On hold**

  Meaning: If something is on hold, no action is being taken.

- **On ice**

  Meaning: If plans are put on ice, they are delayed and no action will be taken for the foreseeable future.

- **On my back**

  Meaning: If people are on your back, they are bothering or nagging you.

- **On my watch**

  Meaning: If something happens on your watch, you are responsible for it as you were in charge.

- **On pins and needles**

  Meaning: If you are on pins and needles, you are very worried about something.

- **On the ball**

  Meaning: If someone's on the ball, they are well-informed and know what's going on in their area of responsibility or interest.

- **On the blink**

  Meaning: Is a machine is on the blink, it isn't working properly or is out of order.
- **On the blower**

  Meaning: If someone is on the blower, they are on the phone.
- **On the cards**

  Meaning: If something is in the cards, it is almost certain to happen.
- **On the cheap**

  Meaning: If you do something on the cheap, you spend as little as possible to do it.
- **On the dole**

  Meaning: Someone receiving financial assistance when unemployed is on the dole.
- **On the dot**

  Meaning: If someone says that they're leaving at seven on the dot, don't be late; they mean at exactly seven o'clock.
- **On the factory floor**

  Meaning: On the factory floor means the place where things are actually produced.
- **On the fiddle**

  Meaning: Someone who is stealing money from work is on the fiddle, especially if they are doing it by fraud.
- **On the flip side**

  Meaning: On the reverse or the other side.
- **On the fly**

  Meaning: If you do things on the fly, you do things without preparation, responding to events as they happen.
- **On the game**

  Meaning: A person who is on the game works as a prostitute.
- **On the ground**

  Meaning: Events on the ground are where things are actually happening, not at a distance.

- **On the hoof**

  Meaning: If you decide something on the hoof, you do it without planning, responding to events as they happen.

- **On the hook**

  Meaning: If someone is on the hook, they are responsible for something.

- **On the house**

  Meaning: If you get something for free that would normally have to be bought, especially in a bar or restaurant, it is on the house.

- **On the knock**

  Meaning: If you buy something on the knock, you pay for it in instalments.

- **On the knocker**

  Meaning: If someone is on the knocker, they are going from house to house trying to buy or sell things or get support.

- **On the lam**

  Meaning: If someone is on the lam, they are hiding from the police or authorities, especially to avoid arrest or prison.

- **On the level**

  Meaning: If someone is honest and trustworthy, they are on the level.

- **On the line**

  Meaning: If somebody's job is on the line, they stand a very good chance of losing it.

- **On the make**

  Meaning: If someone is on the make, they are trying to make a lot of money, usually illegally.

- **On the map**

  Meaning: If a place becomes widely known, it is put on the map. A place that remains unknown is off the map.

- **On the money**

  Meaning: If you are on the money, you are right about something.

- **On the mound**

  Meaning: If you're on the mound, you're on the mound back at your game, back in control.

- **On the never-never**

  Meaning: If you buy something on the never-never, you buy it on long-term credit.

- **On the nod**

  Meaning: If something is accepted by parliament or a committee majority, it is on the nod.

- **On the rebound**

  Meaning: If someone is on the rebound, their relationship has recently ended and they are emotionally unstable.

- **On the right foot**

  Meaning: If you start something or set off on the right foot, you get off to a good start.

- **On the ropes**

  Meaning: When something or someone is on the ropes, it or they are doing badly and likely to fail.

- **On the run**

  Meaning: If someone is on the run, they are avoiding arrest and hiding from the police.

- **On the same page**

  Meaning: If people are on the same page, they have the same information and are thinking the same way.

- **On the same wavelength**

  Meaning: If people are on the same wavelength, they have the same ideas and opinions about something.

- **On the shelf**

  Meaning: If something like a project is on the shelf, nothing is being done about it at the moment.

- **On the skids**

  Meaning: When things or people are on the skids, they are in serious decline and trouble.

- **On the sly**
  Meaning: If someone does something on the sly, they do it furtively or secretly.
- **On the stump**
  Meaning: When politicians are campaigning for support and votes, they are on the stump.
- **On the table**
  Meaning: If a plan or proposal is on the table, it is being discussed.
- **On the take**
  Meaning: Someone who is stealing from work is on the take.
- **On the uptake**
  Meaning: If someone is quick on the uptake, they understand something quickly, but if they're slow on the uptake, it takes them a long time to get it.
- **On the wagon**
  Meaning: If someone is on the wagon, they have stopped drinking alcohol.
- **On top of the world**
  Meaning: If you are on top of the world, everything is going well for you.
- **On your high horse**
  Meaning: When someone is on their high horse, they are being inflexible, arrogant and will not make any compromises.
- **On your last legs**
  Meaning: If someone's on their last legs, they're close to dying.
- **On your soapbox**
  Meaning: If someone is up on their soapbox about something, they are very overtly and verbally passionate about the topic.
- **On your toes**
  Meaning: Someone on his or her toes is alert and ready to go.
- **Once in a blue moon**
  Meaning: If something happens once in a blue moon, it happens very rarely indeed.

- **One arrow, two targets**

  Meaning: To achieve two things with one means.
- **One bad apple**

  Meaning: The full form of this proverb is 'one bad apple spoils the barrel', meaning that a bad person, policy, etc., can ruin everything around it.
- **One doesn't know how to dance and blames it on the stage being uneven**

  Meaning: To blame the means available rather than capability.
- **One for the road**

  Meaning: A last drink before leaving a pub or bar is one for the road.
- **One good turn deserves another**

  Meaning: This means that when people do something good, something good will happen to them.
- **One hand washes the other**

  Meaning: This idiom means that we need other people to get on as cooperation benefits us all.
- **One in the eye**

  Meaning: If you achieve something that will irritate someone because they did not think that you were capable it is one in the eye for them.
- **One man's loss is another man's gain**

  Meaning: This means that one person's setback benefits someone else.
- **One man's meat is another man's poison**

  Meaning: This idiom means that one person can like something very much, but another can hate it.
- **One man's trash is another man's treasure**

  Meaning: What is useless to one person might be valuable to another.
- **One nail drives out another**

  Meaning: A new pain or problem will stop you worrying or feeling bad about something else.

- **One over the eight**
  Meaning: Someone who is one over the eight is drunk.
- **One plus one makes eleven**
  Meaning: Strength in unity.
- **One swallow does not make a summer**
  Meaning: This means that one good or positive event does not mean that everything is all right.
- **One-man band**
  Meaning: If one person does all the work or has all the responsibility somewhere, then they are a one-man band.
- **One-off**
  Meaning: A one-off event only happens once and will not be repeated.
- **One-trick pony**
  Meaning: A one-trick pony is someone who does one thing well, but has limited skills in other areas.
- **Only the wearer knows where the shoe pinches**
  Meaning: This means that it's hard to know how much someone else is suffering.
- **Oops a daisy**
  Meaning: An expression used to indicate surprise.
- **Open all hours**
  Meaning: If a shop or suchlike is open all hours, it only closes, if at all, terribly late.
- **Open book**
  Meaning: If a person is an open book, it is easy to know what they think or how they feel about things.
- **Open old wounds**
  Meaning: If you open old wounds, you revive a quarrel or problem that caused a lot of trouble in the past.
- **Open secret**
  Meaning: An open secret is something that is supposed to be secret but is common knowledge.

- **Pay on the nail**

  Meaning: If you pay on the nail, you pay promptly in cash.
- **Pay peanuts**

  Meaning: If some is paid peanuts, their salary is very low.
- **Pay the piper**

  Meaning: When you pay the piper, you have to accept the consequences of something that you have done wrong or badly.
- **Pay through the nose**

  Meaning: If you pay through the nose for something, you pay a very high price for it.
- **Pay your dues**

  Meaning: If you have paid your dues, you have had your own struggles and earned your place or position.
- **Pen is mightier than the sword**

  Meaning: Words and communication are more powerful than wars and fighting.
- **People person**

  Meaning: Someone who enjoys interacting with people as part of their job.
- **People who live in glass houses should not throw stones**

  Meaning: People should not criticize other people for faults that they have themselves.
- **Perish the thought**

  Meaning: Perish the thought is an expression meaning that you really hope something will not happen.
- **Pet chicken is like lentil**

  Meaning: Not to realize the worth of loved ones.
- **Pet peeve**

  Meaning: A pet peeve is something that irritates an individual greatly.
- **Pick someone's brains**

  Meaning: If you pick someone's brains, you ask them for advice, suggestions and information about something they know about.

- **Pick up the pace**

  Meaning: To speed things up.
- **Pick up the tab**

  Meaning: A person who pays for everyone picks up the tab.
- **Picture perfect**

  Meaning: When something is exactly as it should be it is said to be picture perfect.
- **Pie in the sky**

  Meaning: If an idea or scheme is pie in the sky, it is utterly impractical.
- **Piece of cake**

  Meaning: If something is a piece of cake, it is really easy.
- **Pile it on thick**

  Meaning: To pile it on thick is to exaggerate or overstate something, usually flattery or praise.
- **Pin down with a label**

  Meaning: If you pin someone down with a label, you characterise them, often meant negatively as the label is restrictive.
- **Pin money**

  Meaning: If you work for pin money, you work not because you need to but because it gives you money for extra little luxuries and treats.
- **Pink slip**

  Meaning: If someone receives a pink slip, they receive a letter telling them they have lost their job.
- **Pipe dream**

  Meaning: A pipe dream is an unrealistic, impractical idea or scheme.
- **Piping hot**

  Meaning: If food is piping hot, it is very hot indeed.
- **Place in the sun**

  Meaning: If you have your place in the sun, you find wealth, happiness or whatever you are looking for in life.

- **Plain as the nose on your face**

  Meaning: If something is as plain as the nose on your face, it is very clear and obvious.
- **Plain sailing**

  Meaning: If something is relatively easy and there are no problems doing it, it is plain sailing.
- **Play fast and loose**

  Meaning: If people play fast and loose, they behave in an irresponsible way and don't respect rules, etc.
- **Play for keeps**

  Meaning: If you are playing for keeps, you take things very seriously and the outcome is very important to you; it is not a mere game.
- **Play into someone's hands**

  Meaning: If you play into someone's hands, you do what they were expecting you to do and take advantage of this.
- **Play the field**

  Meaning: Someone who plays the field has sexual relationships with many people.
- **Play the fool**

  Meaning: If someone plays the fool, they behave in a silly way to make people laugh.
- **Play with fire**

  Meaning: If people take foolish risks, they are playing with fire.
- **Playing to the gallery**

  Meaning: If someone plays to the gallery, they say or do things that will make them popular at the expense of more important issues.
- **Please revert**

  Meaning: Please respond tc me if the solution provided is incorrect or insufficient.
- **Pleased as punch**

  Meaning: When someone is pleased as punch, they are very satisfied about something

- **Point the finger**

  Meaning: When you point the finger at someone, you are accusing and blaming them for something.
- **Pointy-heads**

  Meaning: Pointy-heads are supposed intellectuals or experts, but who don't really know that much.
- **Poison pill**

  Meaning: A poison pill is a strategy designed to prevent a company from being take over.
- **Poker face**

  Meaning: Someone with a poker face doesn't show any emotion or reaction so that people don't know what they are feeling.
- **Politically correct**

  Meaning: Things or people that are politically correct use language that will not cause offence.
- **Poor as a church mouse**

  Meaning: If someone is as poor as a church mouse, they are very poor indeed.
- **Pop the question**

  Meaning: When someone pops the question, they ask someone to marry them.
- **Post-haste**

  Meaning: Post-haste means as quickly as possible.
- **Pot calling the kettle black**

  Meaning: If someone hypocritically criticises a person for something that they themselves do, then it is a case of the pot calling the kettle black.
- **Pot-luck**

  Meaning: If you take pot-luck, you take whatever happens to be available at the time.
- **Pour oil on troubled waters**

  Meaning: If someone pours oil on troubled waters, they try to calm things down.

- **Powder your nose**

  Meaning: If somebody goes to powder your nose, it is a euphemism for going to the lavatory (toilet).
- **Practise what you preach**

  Meaning: If you practise what you preach, you do what you say other people should do.
- **Presence of mind**

  Meaning: If someone behaves calmly and rationally in difficult circumstances, they show presence of mind.
- **Pressed for time**

  Meaning: If you are pressed for time, you are in a hurry or working against a very tight schedule.
- **Prick up your ears**

  Meaning: If you prick up your ears, you listen very carefully.
- **Pride goes before a fall**

  Meaning: Excessive pride or confidence can allow people to make mistakes or go wrong.
- **Prim and proper**

  Meaning: Someone who is prim and proper always behaves in the correct way and never breaks the rules of etiquette.
- **Prince charming**

  Meaning: If something is proclaimed from the rooftops, it is made as widely known and as public as possible.
- **Proof of the pudding is in the eating**

  Meaning: This means that something can only be judged when it is tested or by its results.
- **Proud as a peacock**

  Meaning: Someone who is as proud as a peacock is excessively proud.
- **Pull a rabbit out of your hat**

  Meaning: If you pull a rabbit out of a hat, you do something that no one was expecting.

- **Pull in the reins**

  Meaning: When you pull in the reins, you slow down or stop something that has been a bit out of control.
- **Pull out all the stops**

  Meaning: If you pull out all the stops, you do everything you possibly can to achieve the result you want.
- **Pull out of the fire**

  Meaning: If you pull something out of the fire, you save or rescue it.
- **Pull someone's leg**

  Meaning: If you pull someone's leg, you tease them, but not maliciously.
- **Pull strings**

  Meaning: If you pull strings, you use contacts you have got to help you get what you want.
- **Pull the fat from the fire**

  Meaning: If you pull the fat from the fire, you help someone in a difficult situation.
- **Pull the plug**

  Meaning: If the plug is pulled on something like a project, it is terminated prematurely, often by stopping funding.
- **Pull the trigger**

  Meaning: The person who pulls the trigger is the one who does the action that closes or finishes something.
- **Pull up your socks**

  Meaning: If you aren't satisfied with someone and want them to do better, you can tell them to pull up their socks.
- **Pull your finger out!**

  Meaning: If someone tells you to do this, they want you to hurry up.
- **Punching bag**

  Meaning: A punching bag is a person who gets a lot of unfair criticism.

- **Puppy love**

  Meaning: Puppy love is love between two very young people.

- **Push the envelope**

  Meaning: This means to go to the limits, to do something to the maximum possible.

- **Pushing up the daisies**

  Meaning: If someone is said to be pushing up the daisies, they are dead.

- **Put a bug in your ear**

  Meaning: If you put a bug in someone's ear, you give him or her a reminder or suggestion relating to a future event.

- **Put all your eggs in one basket**

  Meaning: If you put all your eggs in one basket, you risk everything on a single opportunity which, like eggs breaking, could go wrong.

- **Put it on the cuff**

  Meaning: If you put something on the cuff, you will take it now and pay for it later.

- **Put lipstick on a pig**

  Meaning: If people put lipstick on a pig, they make superficial or cosmetic changes, hoping that it will make the product more attractive.

- **Put more green into something**

  Meaning: To put more green into something is to spend more or to increase investment in it.

- **Put on airs**

  Meaning: If someone puts on airs, they pretend to be grander and more important than they really are.

- **Put on your thinking cap**

  Meaning: If you put on your thinking cap, you think very hard about something.

- **Put or get someone's back up**

  Meaning: If you put or get someone's back up, you annoy them.

- **Put some dirt on it**

  Meaning: This means that when you get hurt, you should rub it off or shake it off and you'll be ok.

- **Put some mustard on it!**

  Meaning: It's used to encourage someone to throw a ball like a baseball hard or fast.

- **Put somebody's nose out of joint**

  Meaning: If you put someone's nose out of joint, you irritate them or make them angry with you.

- **Put someone on a pedestal**

  Meaning: If you put someone on a pedestal, you admire them greatly, idolise them.

- **Put someone out to pasture**

  Meaning: If someone is put out to pasture, they are forced to resign or give up some responsibilities.

- **Put that in your pipe and smoke it**

  Meaning: This is used as an unsympathetic way of telling someone to accept what you have just said.

- **Put the carriage before the horse**

  Meaning: If you put the carriage before the horse, you try to do things in the wrong order.

- **Put the kybosh on**

  Meaning: To put an end to something.

- **Put the pedal to the metal**

  Meaning: If you put the pedal to the metal, you go faster.

- **Put to the sword**

  Meaning: If someone is put to the sword, he or she is killed or executed.

- **Put two and two together**

  Meaning: If someone puts two and two together, they reach a correct conclusion from the evidence.

- **Put up or shut up**

  Meaning: 'Put up or shut up' means you do something you are talking about or not to talk about it anymore.

- **Put you in mind**

  Meaning: If something suggests something to you, it puts you in mind of that thing.

- **Put you in the picture**

  Meaning: If you put someone in the picture, you tell them the information they need to know about something.

- **Put your hand on your heart**

  Meaning: If you can out your hand on your heart, then you can say something knowing it to be true.

- **Put your shoulder to the wheel**

  Meaning: When you put your shoulder to the wheel, you contribute to an effort.

- **Put yourself in someone's shoes**

  Meaning: If you put yourself in someone's shoes, you imagine what it is like to be in their position.

- **Putting the cart before the horse**

  Meaning: When you put the cart before the horse, you are doing something the wrong way round.

Q

- **Quart into a pint pot**

  Meaning: If you try to put or get a quart into a pint pot, you try to put too much in a small space.

- **Queen bee**

  Meaning: The queen bee is a woman who holds the most important position in a place.

- **Queen of Hearts**

  Meaning: A woman who is pre-eminent in her area is a Queen of Hearts.

- **Queer your pitch**

  Meaning: If someone queers your pitch, they interfere in your affairs and spoil things.

- **Question of time**

  Meaning: If something's a question of time, it's certain to happen, though we don't know exactly when.
- **Queue jumping**

  Meaning: Someone who goes to the front of a queue instead of waiting is jumping the queue.
- **Quick as a flash**

  Meaning: If something happens quick as a flash, it happens very fast indeed.
- **Quick buck**

  Meaning: If you make some money easily, you make a quick buck.
- **Quick fix**

  Meaning: A quick fix is an easy solution, especially one that will not last.
- **Quick off the mark**

  Meaning: If someone is quick off the mark, they are very quick to use, start or do something new.
- **Quick on the trigger**

  Meaning: Someone who is quick on the trigger acts or responds quickly.
- **Quids in**

  Meaning: If somebody is quids in, they stand to make a lot of money from something.
- **Quiet as a cat**

  Meaning: If somebody is as quiet as a cat they make as little noise as possible and try to be unnoticeable.
- **Quiet as a mouse**

  Meaning: If someone's as quiet as a mouse, they make absolutely no noise.
- **Quiet before the Storm**

  Meaning: When you know that something is about to go horribly wrong, but hasn't just yet, then you are in the quiet before the storm.

- **Quitters never win; winners never quit**

  Meaning: If you quit you will never get what you want, but if you keep trying you will find a way to get what you want.

R

- **Rack your brain**

  Meaning: If you rack your brain, you think very hard when trying to remember something.

- **Rags to riches**

  Meaning: Someone who starts life very poor and becomes rich goes from rags to riches.

- **Rain on your parade**

  Meaning: If someone rains on your parade, they ruin your pleasure or your plans.

- **Raining cats and dogs**

  Meaning: When it is raining cats and dogs, it is raining very heavily.

- **Rainy day**

  Meaning: If you save something, especially money, for a rainy day, you save it for some possible problem or trouble in the future.

- **Raise eyebrows**

  Meaning: If something raises eyebrows, it shocks or surprises people.

- **Rake over old coals**

  Meaning: If you go back to old problems and try to bring them back, making trouble for someone, you are raking over old coals.

- **Rank and file**

  Meaning: The rank and file are the ordinary members of a company, organization, etc., excluding the managers and directors.

- **Rat race**

  Meaning: The rat race is the ruthless, competitive struggle for success in work, etc.

- **Raw deal**

  Meaning: If you get a raw deal, you are treated unfairly.
- **Read from the same page**

  Meaning: When people are reading from the same page, they say the same things in public about an issue.
- **Read someone the riot act**

  Meaning: If you read someone the riot act, you give them a clear warning that if they don't stop doing something, they will be in serious trouble.
- **Real deal**

  Meaning: If something is the real deal, it is genuine and good.
- **Real trouper**

  Meaning: A real trouper is someone who will fight for what they believe in and doesn't give up easily.
- **Recharge your batteries**

  Meaning: If you recharge your batteries, you do something to regain your energy after working hard for a long time.
- **Red carpet**

  Meaning: If you give someone the red-carpet treatment, you give them a special welcome to show that you think they are important. You can roll out the red carpet, too.
- **Red herring**

  Meaning: If something is a distraction from the real issues, it is a red herring.
- **Red letter day**

  Meaning: A red letter day is a one of good luck, when something special happens to you.
- **Red light district**

  Meaning: The red light district is the area of a town or city where there is prostitution, sex shops, etc.
- **Red mist**

  Meaning: If someone sees red or the red mist, they lose their temper and self-control completely.

- **Red rag to a bull**

  Meaning: If something is a red rag to a bull, it is something that will inevitably make somebody angry or cross.

- **Red tape**

  Meaning: This is a negative term for the official paperwork and bureaucracy that we have to deal with.

- **Reds under the bed**

  Meaning: An ironic allusion to the obsession some people have that there are reds (communists) everywhere plotting violent revolution.

- **Reduce to ashes**

  Meaning: If something is reduced to ashes, it is destroyed or made useless. His infidelities reduced their relationship to ashes.

- **Rest is gravy**

  Meaning: If the rest is gravy, it is easy and straightforward once you have reached that stage.

- **Revenge is sweet**

  Meaning: When you are happy to be proved right, then you know that revenge is sweet.

- **Rewrite history**

  Meaning: If you rewrite history, you change your version of past events so as to make yourself look better than you would if the truth was told.

- **Rhyme or reason**

  Meaning: If something is without rhyme or reason, it is unreasonable.

- **Rib tickler**

  Meaning: A rib tickler is a story or joke that will make you laugh a lot.

- **Rich man's family**

  Meaning: A rich man's family consists of one son and one daughter.

- **Ride for a fall**

  Meaning: If someone is riding for a fall, they are taking great risks that are likely to end in a disaster.

- **Ride high**

  Meaning: If someone is riding high, they are very successful at the moment.

- **Ride roughshod**

  Meaning: If someone rides roughshod over other people, they impose their will without caring at all for other people's feelings.

- **Ride with the tide**

  Meaning: If you ride with the tide, you accept the majority decision.

- **Right as rain**

  Meaning: If things are right as rain, then everything is going well in your life.

- **Right church, wrong pew**

  Meaning: Right church, wrong pew means that someone is very nearly right, but someting is wrong.

- **Right royal**

  Meaning: A right royal night out would be an extremely exciting, memorable and fun one.

- **Right up your street**

  Meaning: If something is ideal for you, it is right up your street.

- **Ringside seat**

  Meaning: If you have a ringside seat, you can observe something from a very close and clear position.

- **Rise and shine**

  Meaning: If you wake up full of energy, you rise and shine.

- **Rise from the ashes**

  Meaning: If something rises from the ashes, it recovers after a serious failure.

- **Rob the cradle**

  Meaning: To rob the cradle is to marry or have a relationship with someone much younger.

- **Roll out the red carpet**

  Meaning: If you roll out the red carpet, you treat someone in a special way, especially when welcoming them.

- **Roll the dice**

  Meaning: To take a chance on something.

- **Roll with the punches**

  Meaning: If you roll with the punches, you are flexible and able to adapt to difficult circumstances.

- **Rolling in money**

  Meaning: If someone has a lot of money, more than they could possibly need, they are rolling in money.

- **Rolling in the aisles**

  Meaning: If the audience watching something are laughing loudly, the show has them rolling in the aisles.

- **Rooted to the spot**

  Meaning: If someone is rooted to the spot, they cannot move, either physically or they cannot think their way out of a problem.

- **Rose-coloured glasses**

  Meaning: If people see things through rose-coloured glasses, they see them in a more positive light than they really are.

- **Rough around the edges**

  Meaning: If someone is rough around the edges, they haven't mastered something, though they show promise.

- **Rough diamond**

  Meaning: A rough diamond is a person who might be a bit rude but who is good underneath it all.

- **Rough edges**

  Meaning: If something has rough edges, it is still not a finished product and not all of a uniform standard.

- **Rough patch**

  Meaning: A rough patch is a difficult or trying period.

- **Rough-hewn**

  Meaning: If something, especially something made from wood or stone, is rough-hewn, it is unfinished or unpolished.

- **Round the houses**

  Meaning: If you go round the houses, you do something in an inefficient way when there is a quicker, more convenient way.

- **Rub shoulders**

  Meaning: If you rub shoulders with people, you meet and spend time with them, especially when they are powerful or famous.

- **Rub someone up the wrong way**

  Meaning: If you annoy or irritate someone when you didn't mean to, you rub them up the wrong way.

- **Rudderless ship**

  Meaning: If an organization, company, government, etc., is like a rudderless ship, it has no clear direction and drifts about without reaching its goals.

- **Rue the day**

  Meaning: This means that the person will one day bitterly regret what they have done.

- **Ruffle a few feathers**

  Meaning: If you ruffle a few feathers, you annoy some people when making changes or improvements.

- **Rule of thumb**

  Meaning: Rule of thumb means approximately.

- **Rule the roost**

  Meaning: If someone rules the roost they are the boss.

- **Run around the bush**

  Meaning: If you run around the bush, it means that you're taking a long time to get to the point.

- **Run circles around someone**

  Meaning: If you can run circles around someone, you are smarter and intellectually quicker than they are.

- **Run into the sand**

  Meaning: If something runs into the sand, it fails to achieve a result.
- **Run it up the flagpole and see if anyone salutes**

  Meaning: This idiom is used to suggest trying out an idea to see if people accept it.
- **Run off your feet**

  Meaning: If you are run off your feet, you are extremely busy and don't have enough time to do everything.
- **Run out of gas**

  Meaning: If a campaign, project, etc., runs out of gas, it loses energy and momentum, and progress slows or halts.
- **Run rings around someone**

  Meaning: If you run rings around someone, you are so much better than them that they have no chance of keeping up with you.
- **Run something into the ground**

  Meaning: If people run something into the ground, they treat or manage it so badly that they ruin it.
- **Run the gauntlet**

  Meaning: If somebody is being criticised harshly by a lot of people, they are said to run the gauntlet.
- **Run the show**

  Meaning: If someone runs the show, they like to be in control and make all the decisions.
- **Run to ground**

  Meaning: If you run someone or something to ground, you pursue until you capture or find them or it.
- **Run with the hare and hunt with the hounds**

  Meaning: This means to be a member of or to support two groups that are at odds with each other.
- **Run your mouth off**

  Meaning: If someone runs their mouth off, they talk too much.

- **Run-of-the-mill**

  Meaning: If something is run-of-the-mill, there is nothing exceptional about it– it is ordinary or average.

- **Running on empty**

  Meaning: If you are exhausted but keep going, you are running on empty.

S

- **Sacred cow**

  Meaning: Something that is a sacred cow is held in such respect that it cannot be criticised or attacked.

- **Safe and sound**

  Meaning: If you arrive safe and sound, then nothing has harmed you on your way.

- **Safe as houses**

  Meaning: Something that is as safe as houses is very secure or certain.

- **Safe bet**

  Meaning: A proposition that is a safe bet doesn't have any risks attached.

- **Safe pair of hands**

  Meaning: A person who can be trusted to do something without causing any trouble is a safe pair of hands.

- **Safety in numbers**

  Meaning: If a lot of people do something risky at the same time, the risk is reduced because there is safety in numbers.

- **Sail under false colours**

  Meaning: Someone who sails under false colours is hypocritical or pretends to be something they aren't in order to deceive people.

- **Salt of the earth**

  Meaning: People who are salt of the earth are decent, dependable and unpretentious.

- **Same old, same old**

  Meaning: When nothing changes, it's the same old, same old.
- **Save face**

  Meaning: If someone saves face, they manage to protect their reputation.
- **Save your skin**

  Meaning: If someone saves their skin, they manage to avoid getting into serious trouble.
- **Saved by the bell**

  Meaning: If you are saved by the bell, you are rescued from a danger or a tricky situation just in time.
- **Saving grace**

  Meaning: If someone has some character defects, but has a characteristic that compensate for their failings and shortcomings, this is their saving grace.
- **Saying is one thing; doing is another**

  Meaning: It's harder to do something than it is to say that you will do it.
- **Scales fall from your eyes**

  Meaning: When the scales fall from your eyes, you suddenly realise the truth about something.
- **Scare the daylights out of someone**

  Meaning: If you scare the daylights out of someone, you terrify them.
- **Scattered to the four winds**

  Meaning: If something's scattered to the four winds, it goes out in all directions.
- **Scent blood**

  Meaning: If you can scent blood, you feel that a rival is having difficulties and you are going to beat them.
- **Scratch the surface**

  Meaning: When you scratch the surface of something, you have a superficial knowledge or understanding of it.

- **Scream blue murder**

  Meaning: If someone shouts very loudly in anger, or fear, they scream blue murder.
- **Screw loose**

  Meaning: If someone has a screw loose, they are crazy.
- **Screwed if you do, screwed if you don't**

  Meaning: This means that no matter what you decide or do in a situation, there will be negative consequences.
- **Sea change**

  Meaning: An expression that connotes big change; a significant change in comparison to a minor, trivial or insignificant change.
- **Sea legs**

  Meaning: If you are getting your sea legs, it takes you a while to get used to something new.
- **Seamy side**

  Meaning: The seamy side of something is the unpleasant or sordid aspect it has.
- **Searching question**

  Meaning: A searching question goes straight to the heart of the subject matter, possibly requiring an answer with a degree of honesty that the other person finds uncomfortable.
- **Second thoughts**

  Meaning: If some has second thoughts, they start to think that an idea, etc., is not as good as it sounded at first and are starting to have doubts.
- **Second wind**

  Meaning: If you overcome tiredness and find new energy and enthusiasm, you have second wind.
- **See eye to eye**

  Meaning: If people see eye to eye, they agree about everything.
- **See red**

  Meaning: If someone sees red, they become very angry about something.

- **See the elephant**

  Meaning: If you see the elephant, you experience much more than you wish to; it is often used when a soldier goes into a warzone for the first time.
- **See the light**

  Meaning: When someone sees the light, they realise the truth.
- **See you later**

  Meaning: A casual way of saying to friends I'll see you again, sometime.
- **See you on the big drum**

  Meaning: A good night phrase to children.
- **Seed money**

  Meaning: Seed money is money that is used to start a small business.
- **Seeing is believing**

  Meaning: This idiom means that people can only really believe what they experience personally.
- **Sell down the river**

  Meaning: If you sell someone down the river, you betray their trust.
- **Sell like hot cakes**

  Meaning: If a product is selling very well, it is selling like hot cakes.
- **Sell your soul**

  Meaning: If someone sells their soul, their betray the most precious beliefs.
- **Send someone packing**

  Meaning: If you send someone packing, you send them away, normally when they want something from you.
- **Separate the sheep from the goats**

  Meaning: If you separate the sheep from the goats, you sort out the good from the bad.

- **Separate the wheat from the chaff**
  Meaning: Select what is useful or valuable and reject what is useless or worthless.
- **Serve time**
  Meaning: When someone is serving time, they are in prison.
- **Set a thief to catch a thief**
  Meaning: The best person to catch a criminal is another criminal as they understand how criminals work.
- **Set in stone**
  Meaning: If something is set in stone, it cannot be changed or altered.
- **Set the stage**
  Meaning: If you create the conditions for something to happen or take place, you set the stage for it.
- **Set the wheels in motion**
  Meaning: When you set the wheels in motion, you get something started.
- **Set your sights on**
  Meaning: If you set your sights on someone or something, it is your ambition to beat them or to achieve that goal.
- **Seven sheets to the wind**
  Meaning: If someone is seven sheets to the wind, they are very drunk.
- **Seventh heaven**
  Meaning: If you are in seventh heaven, you are extremely happy.
- **Shaggy dog story**
  Meaning: A shaggy dog story is a joke which is a long story with a silly end.
- **Shake a leg**
  Meaning: If you shake a leg, you are out of bed and active. It can be used to tell someone to hurry up.
- **Shape up or ship out**
  Meaning: If someone has to shape up or ship out, they have to improve or leave their job, organization, etc.

- **Sharp cookie**
  Meaning: Someone who isn't easily deceived or fooled is a sharp cookie.
- **Shed light**
  Meaning: If you shed light on something, you make it clearer and easier to understand.
- **Shifting sands**
  Meaning: If the sands are shifting, circumstances are changing.
- **Shilly-shally**
  Meaning: If people shilly-shally, they can't make up their minds about something and put off the decision.
- **Ship came in**
  Meaning: If your ship has come in, something very good has happened to you.
- **Shoe is on the other foot**
  Meaning: If the shoe is on the other foot, someone is experiencing what they used to make others experience, normally negative things.
- **Shoot from the hip**
  Meaning: Someone who shoots from the hip talks very directly or insensitively without thinking beforehand.
- **Shoot the breeze**
  Meaning: When you shoot the breeze, you chat in a relaxed way.
- **Shoot your wad**
  Meaning: When you have shot your wad, you have expended everything and have no more to say or do about a matter.
- **Shoot yourself in the foot**
  Meaning: If you shoot yourself in the foot, you do something that damages your ambition, career, etc.
- **Shooting fish in a barrel**
  Meaning: If something is like shooting fish in a barrel, it is so easy that success is guaranteed.

- **Shop floor**

  Meaning: 'Shop floor' refers to the part of an organization where the work is actually performed rather than just managed.
- **Short end of the stick**

  Meaning: If someone gets the short end of the stick, they are unfairly treated or don't get what they deserve.
- **Short horse soon curried**

  Meaning: A convenient and superficial explanation that is normally unconvincing is a short horse soon curried.
- **Short shrift**

  Meaning: If somebody gives you short shrift, they treat you rudely and brusquely, showing no interest or sympathy.
- **Short-change**

  Meaning: If you are short-changed, someone cheats you of money or doesn't give you full value for something.
- **Shot across the bow**

  Meaning: A shot across the bow is a warning to tell someone to stop doing something or face very serious consequences.
- **Shot in the dark**

  Meaning: If you have a shot in the dark at something, you try something where you have little hope of success.
- **Show someone a clean pair of heels**

  Meaning: If you show someone a clean pair of heels, you run faster than them when they are chasing you.
- **Show someone the ropes**

  Meaning: If you show someone the ropes, you explain to someone new how things work and how to do a job.
- **Show your true colours**

  Meaning: To show your true colours is to reveal yourself as you really are.
- **Sick as a parrot**

  Meaning: If someone's sick as a parrot about something, they are unhappy, disappointed or depressed about it.

- **Sick to death**

  Meaning: If you are sick to death of something, you have been exposed to so much of it that you cannot take anymore.
- **Sight for sore eyes**

  Meaning: Someone or something that is a sight for sore eyes is a pleasure to see.
- **Signed, sealed and delivered**

  Meaning: If something's signed, sealed and delivered, it has been done correctly, following all the necessary procedures.
- **Silence is golden**

  Meaning: It is often better to say nothing than to talk, so silence is golden.
- **Silver bullet**

  Meaning: A silver bullet is a complete solution to a large problem, a solution that seems magical.
- **Silver screen**

  Meaning: The silver screen is the cinema.
- **Silver surfer**

  Meaning: A silver surfer is an elderly person who uses the internet.
- **Sing for your supper**

  Meaning: If you have to sing for your supper, you have to work to get the pay or reward you need or want.
- **Sing like a canary**

  Meaning: If someone sings like a canary, they tell everything they know about a crime or wrongdoing to the police or authorities.
- **Sink or swim**

  Meaning: Of you are left to sink or swim, no one gives you any help and it's up to you whether you fail or succeed.
- **Sit on the fence**

  Meaning: If someone sits on the fence, they try not to support either side in a dispute.

- **Sit pretty**

  Meaning: Someone who's sitting pretty is in a very advantageous situation.
- **Sit well with**

  Meaning: If something doesn't sit well with you, it doesn't please you or is not acceptable to you.
- **Sitting duck**

  Meaning: A sitting duck is something or someone that is easy to criticise or target.
- **Six feet under**

  Meaning: If someone is six feet under, they are dead.
- **Sixes and sevens**

  Meaning: If something is all at sixes and sevens, then there is a lot of disagreement and confusion about what should be done.
- **Skate on thin ice**

  Meaning: If someone is skating on thin ice, they are taking a big risk.
- **Skeleton in the closet**

  Meaning: If someone has a skeleton in the closet, they have a dark, shameful secret in their past that they want to remain secret.
- **Skin and bones**

  Meaning: If someone is skin and bones, they are very underweight and look bad.
- **Skin in the game**

  Meaning: A person who has skin in the game has invested in the company they are running.
- **Skin someone alive**

  Meaning: If someone skins you alive, they admonish and punish you hard.
- **Sky is the limit**

  Meaning: When people say that the sky is the limit, they think that there are no limits to the possibilities something could have.

- **Slap on the wrist**

  Meaning: If someone gets a slap on the wrist, they get a very minor punishment when they could have been punished more severely.
- **Sleep like a baby**

  Meaning: If you sleep very well, you sleep like a baby.
- **Sleep like a log**

  Meaning: If you sleep like a log, you sleep very soundly.
- **Sleight of hand**

  Meaning: Sleight of hand is the ability to use your hands in a clever way, like a magician performing tricks you can't see.
- **Slim chance**

  Meaning: A slim chance is a very small chance.
- **Sling your hook**

  Meaning: This is used as a way of telling someone to leave or go away.
- **Slip of the tongue**

  Meaning: If you say something accidentally, it is a slip of the tongue.
- **Slip through one's fingers**

  Meaning: If something slips through one's fingers it escapes or is lost through carelessness.
- **Slip through the net**

  Meaning: If something slips through the net, it isn't noticed or avoids detection.
- **Slippery slope**

  Meaning: A slippery slope is where a measure would lead to further worse measures.
- **Slough of despond**

  Meaning: If someone is very depressed or in despair, they're in a slough of despond.
- **Slow but sure**

  Meaning: If something or someone is slow but sure, they may take their time to do something, but they are reliable.

- **Slowly, slowly catchy monkey**

  Meaning: This means that eventually you will achieve your goal.
- **Smack in the face**

  Meaning: If something is a smack in the face, it is a shock, usually one that impedes progress.
- **Small beer**

  Meaning: If something is small beer, it's unimportant.
- **Small dog, tall weeds**

  Meaning: This idiom is used to describe someone the speaker does not believe has the ability or resources to handle a task or job.
- **Small potatoes**

  Meaning: Someone or something that is unimportant is small potatoes.
- **Smart as a whip**

  Meaning: A person who is smart as a whip is very clever.
- **Smarty pants**

  Meaning: A smarty pants is someone who displays the intelligence in an annoying way.
- **Smell a rat**

  Meaning: If you smell a rat, you know instinctively that something is wrong or that someone is lying to you.
- **Smoke and mirrors**

  Meaning: An attempt to conceal something is smoke and mirrors.
- **Smoke like a chimney**

  Meaning: Someone who smokes very heavily smokes like a chimney.
- **Smoking gun**

  Meaning: A smoking gun is definitive proof of someone's guilt.
- **Snake in the grass**

  Meaning: Someone who is a snake in the grass betrays you even though you have trusted them.

- **Snake of the sleeve**

  Meaning: The deceitful is very closely related or known.
- **Snake oil**

  Meaning: Advice or medicine which is of no use.
- **Snug as a bug in a rug**

  Meaning: If you're as snug as a bug in a rug, you are feeling very comfortable indeed.
- **So it goes**

  Meaning: This idiom is used to be fatalistic and accepting when something goes wrong.
- **So on and so forth**

  Meaning: And so on and so forth mean the same as etcetera (etc.).
- **Sod's law**

  Meaning: Sod's law states that if something can go wrong then it will.
- **Soft soap someone**

  Meaning: If you soft soap someone, you flatter them.
- **Something nasty in the woodshed**

  Meaning: Something nasty in the woodshed means that someone as a dark secret or an unpleasant experience in their past.
- **Sound as a bell**

  Meaning: If something or someone is as sound as a bell, they are very healthy or in very good condition.
- **Sour grapes**

  Meaning: When someone says something critical or negative because they are jealous, it is a case of sour grapes.
- **Sow the seeds**

  Meaning: When people sow the seeds, they start something that will have a much greater impact in the future.
- **Spare the rod and spoil the child**

  Meaning: This means that if you don't discipline children, they will become spoilt.

- **Speak of the devil!**

  Meaning: If you are talking about someone and they happen to walk in, you can use this idiom as a way of letting them know you were talking about them.

T

- **Tables are turned**

  Meaning: A change in situation, giving the advantage to the party who had previously been at a disadvantage.
- **Tackle an issue**

  Meaning: If you tackle an issue or problem, you resolve or deal with it.
- **Take a leaf out of someone's book**

  Meaning: If you take a leaf out of someone's book, you copy something they do because it will help you.
- **Take a punch**

  Meaning: If somebody takes a blow, something bad happens to them.
- **Take aback**

  Meaning: If you are taken aback, it means that you're surprised or shocked by something.
- **Take for a test drive**

  Meaning: If you take something for a test driver, you try something to see if you like it.
- **Take it in your stride**

  Meaning: If you take something in your stride, you deal with it even though it is difficult or unpleasant without letting it bother or upset you.
- **Take no prisoners**

  Meaning: If people take no prisoners, they do things in a very aggressive way, without considering any harm they might do to achieve their objectives.
- **Take one for the team**

  Meaning: To sacrifice oneself in some way for the good of the group.

- **Take sand to the beach**

  Meaning: Doing something that is completely pointless or unnecessary is like taking sand to the beach.
- **Take someone for a ride**

  Meaning: If you are taken for a ride, you are deceived by someone.
- **Take someone to task**

  Meaning: If you take someone to task, you scold them for something they have done wrong.
- **Take stock**

  Meaning: To assess a situation, to conduct a personal inventory of ones beliefs and values, etc.
- **Take the cake**

  Meaning: If something takes the cake, it is the best and takes the honours.
- **Take the flak**

  Meaning: If you take the flak, you are strongly criticised for something.
- **Take the floor**

  Meaning: Start talking or giving a speech to a group.
- **Take the heat**

  Meaning: If you take the heat, you take the criticism or blame for something you didn't do, normally to protect the guilty person.
- **Take your breath away**

  Meaning: If something takes your breath away, it astonishes or surprises you.
- **Take your eye off the ball**

  Meaning: If someone takes their eye off the ball, they don't concentrate on something important that they should be looking at.
- **Take your hat off**

  Meaning: If you say that you take your hat off to someone, you are showing your respect or admiration.

- **Take your hat off to somebody**

  Meaning: If you take your hat off to someone, you acknowledge that they have done something exceptional or otherwise deserve your respect.

- **Take your medicine**

  Meaning: If you take your medicine, you accept the consequences of something you have done wrong.

- **Talk a glass eye to sleep**

  Meaning: Someone who could talk a glass eye to sleep is very boring and repetitive.

- **Talk is cheap**

  Meaning: It's easy to talk about something but harder to actually do it.

- **Talk nineteen to the dozen**

  Meaning: If someone talks very quickly, they talk nineteen to the dozen.

- **Talk of the town**

  Meaning: When everybody is talking about particular people and events, they are he talk of the town.

- **Talk out of the back of your head**

  Meaning: If someone is talking out of the back of their head, they are talking rubbish.

- **Talk shop**

  Meaning: If you talk shop, you talk about work matters, especially if you do this outside work.

- **Talk the hind legs off a donkey**

  Meaning: A person who is excessively or extremely talkative can talk the hind legs off a donkey.

- **Talk turkey**

  Meaning: When people talk turkey, they discuss something frankly.

- **Talk your arm off**

  Meaning: Someone who talks so much that it is a strain to listen can talk your arm off.

- **Talking to a brick wall**

  Meaning: If you talk to someone and they do not listen to you, it is like talking to a brick wall.
- **Tall drink of water**

  Meaning: Someone who is very tall and slender is a tall drink of water.
- **Tall order**

  Meaning: Something that is likely to be hard to achieve or fulfill is a tall order.
- **Taste blood**

  Meaning: If someone has tasted blood, they have achieved something and are encouraged to think that victory is within their grasp.
- **Teacher's pet**

  Meaning: The teacher's favourite pupil is the teacher's pet, especially if disliked by the other pupils.
- **Tear your hair out**

  Meaning: If someone is tearing their hair out, they are extremely worried or agitated about something.
- **Tell it to the marines**

  Meaning: People use this expression when they don't believe someone.
- **Tempest in a teapot**

  Meaning: If people exaggerate the seriousness of a situation or problem, they are making a tempest in a teapot.
- **Ten a penny**

  Meaning: If something is ten a penny, it is very common.
- **That ship has sailed**

  Meaning: A particular opportunity has passed you by when that ship has sailed.
- **That's all she wrote**

  Meaning: This idiom is used to show that something has ended and there is nothing more to say about something.

- **That which runs is called a car**
  Meaning: When the things are running smoothly, let it be.
- **The apple does not fall far from the tree**
  Meaning: Offspring grow up to be like their parents.
- **The ayes have it**
  Meaning: If the ayes have it, those who voted in favour of something have won.
- **The ball's in your court**
  Meaning: If somebody says this to you, they mean that it's up to you to decide or take the next step.
- **The cat's meow**
  Meaning: If something is the cat's meow, it's excellent.
- **The common weal**
  Meaning: If something is done for the common weal, it is done in the interests and for the benefit of the majority or the general public.
- **The dough is runny in poverty**
  Meaning: In adversity, everything takes a bad turn.
- **The fruit of patience is sweet**
  Meaning: Patience is virtue.
- **The ghost of feet don't agree to talks**
  Meaning: Those who are stubborn will not be easily convinced by logical talking.
- **The horn on the head of a donkey vanishes**
  Meaning: To be missing.
- **The line forms on the right**
  Meaning: Something's meaning is becoming clear when the line forms on the right.
- **The long and short**
  Meaning: The long and short of something is the substance, the most important part or the gist.
- **The penny dropped**
  Meaning: When the penny drops, someone belatedly

understands something that everyone else has long since understood.

- **The plot thickens**

  Meaning: When the plot thickens, a situation become more complicated and difficult.
- **The short straw**

  Meaning: If you take the short straw, you lose a selection process, which means that you have to do something unpleasant.
- **The sun might rise in the west**

  Meaning: When people say this, they mean that they don't expect something to happen.
- **The thief scolds the police officer**

  Meaning: Offence is the best defense.
- **Their bark is worse than their bite**

  Meaning: If someone's bark is worse than their bite, they get angry and shout and make threats, but don't actually do anything.
- **There are many ways to skin a cat**

  Meaning: This is an expression meaning there are many different ways of doing the same thing.
- **There's a dead cat on the line**

  Meaning: This used as a way of telling people that something suspicious is happening.
- **There's delay in god's house not darkness**

  Meaning: All is fair in life even if there are slight delays.
- **There's delay in his house but not injustice**

  Meaning: In god's house there might be delay in serving justice but never overlooked.
- **There's something black in the lentil**

  Meaning: Something is fishy.
- **There's the rub**

  Meaning: The meaning of this idiom is 'that's the problem'.
- **Thick and fast**

  Meaning: If things are happening thick and fast, they are happening so fast they seemed to be joined together.

- **Thick as mince**

  Meaning: If someone is as thick as mince, they are very stupid indeed.
- **Thick as thieves**

  Meaning: If people are thick as thieves, they are very close friends who have no secrets from each other.
- **Thick-skinned**

  Meaning: If a person is thick-skinned, they are not affected by criticism.
- **Thieves are cousins**

  Meaning: Evil attracts evil.
- **Thin as a rake**

  Meaning: A rake is a garden tool with a long, thin, wooden handle, so someone very thin is thin as a rake.
- **Thin end of the wedge**

  Meaning: The thin end of the wedge is something small and seemingly unimportant that will lead to something much bigger and more serious.
- **Thin line**

  Meaning: If there's a thin line between things, it's hard to distinguish them- there's a thin line between love and hate.
- **Thin-skinned**

  Meaning: If somebody is thin-skinned, they are very sensitive to any sort of criticism.
- **Think outside the box**

  Meaning: If you think outside the box, you think in an imaginative and creative way.
- **Think the world of**

  Meaning: To hold something or someone in very high esteem. To love or admire immensely.
- **Third time's the charm**

  Meaning: This is used when the third time one tries something, one achieves a successful outcome.

- **Thorn in your side**

  Meaning: A thorn in your side is someone or something that causes trouble or makes life difficult for you.

- **Those who are drowning get help of a twig**

  Meaning: Even the smallest of the thing can help those in dire need.

- **Those who thunder don't pour**

  Meaning: Those who talk don't perform.

- **Three sheets to the wind**

  Meaning: If someone is three sheets to the wind, they are drunk.

- **Thrilled to bits**

  Meaning: If you are thrilled to bits, you are extremely pleased or excited about something.

- **Through the ceiling**

  Meaning: If prices go through the ceiling, they rise very quickly.

- **Through the floor**

  Meaning: If prices go, or fall, through the floor, they fall very quickly.

- **Through thick and thin**

  Meaning: If someone supports you through thick and thin, they support you during good times and bad.

- **Throw a monkey wrench into the works**

  Meaning: If you throw a monkey wrench into the works, you ensure that something fails.

- **Throw a sickie**

  Meaning: If you pretend to be ill to take a day off work or school, you throw a sickie.

- **Throw a spanner in the works**

  Meaning: If you throw a spanner in the works, you cause a problem that stops or slows progress on something that was going well.

- **Throw caution to the wind**

  Meaning: When people throw caution to the wind, they take a great risk.

- **Throw in the towel**

  Meaning: If you throw in the towel, you admit that you are defeated or cannot do something.

- **Throw someone a line**

  Meaning: If someone throws you a line, they give you help when you are in serious difficulties.

- **Throw someone to the wolves**

  Meaning: If someone is thrown to the wolves, they are abandoned and have to face trouble without any support.

- **Throw someone under the bus**

  Meaning: To throw someone under the bus is to get the person in trouble either by placing blame on that person or not standing up for him.

- **Throw the baby out with the bath water**

  Meaning: If you get rid of useful things when discarding inessential things, you throw the baby out with the bath water.

- **Throw the book at someone**

  Meaning: If you throw the book at someone, you punish them as severely as possible.

- **Thumb your nose at**

  Meaning: If you thumb your nose at something, you reject it or scorn it.

- **Thumbs down and thumbs up**

  Meaning: If something gets the thumbs up, it gets approval, while the thumbs down means disapproval.

- **Tickle your fancy**

  Meaning: If something tickles your fancy, it appeals to you and you want to try it or have it.

- **Tickled pink**

  Meaning: If you are very pleased about something, you are tickled pink.

- **Tie the knot**

  Meaning: When people tie the knot, they get married.

- **Tight rein**

  Meaning: If things or people are kept on a tight rein, they are given very little freedom or controlled carefully.
- **Tight ship**

  Meaning: If you run a tight ship, you control an organization or business firmly to maximise performance.
- **Tighten your belt**

  Meaning: If you have to tighten your belt, you have to economise.
- **Till the cows come home**

  Meaning: This idioms means 'for a very long time'.
- **Till you're blue in the face**

  Meaning: If you do something till you're blue in the face, you do it repeatedly without achieving the desired result until you're incredibly frustrated.
- **Tilt at windmills**

  Meaning: A person who tilts at windmills, tries to do things that will never work in practice.
- **Time and again**

  Meaning: If something happens time and again, it happens repeatedly.
- **Time does sail**

  Meaning: This idioms means that time passes by unnoticed.
- **Time flies**

  Meaning: This idiom means that time moves quickly and often unnoticed.
- **Time is on my side**

  Meaning: If time is on your side, you have the luxury of not having to worry about how long something will take.
- **Time of your life**

  Meaning: If you're having the time of your life, you are enjoying yourself very much indeed.
- **Tip of the iceberg**

  Meaning: Part of a problem that can be seen, with far more serious problems lying underneath.

- **Tit for tat**

  Meaning: If someone responds to an insult by being rude back, it's tit for tat– repaying something negative the same way.
- **To a fault**

  Meaning: If something does something to a fault, they do it excessively. So someone who is generous to a fault is too generous.
- **To a man**

  Meaning: If a group of people does, believes, thinks, etc., something to a man, then they all do it.
- **To all intents and purposes**

  Meaning: This means in all the most important ways.
- **To be as thick as two bricks**

  Meaning: Someone who is as thick as two bricks is really stupid.
- **To be born with a silver spoon in the mouth**

  Meaning: To be born rich.
- **To be dog cheap**

  Meaning: If something's dog cheap, it is very cheap indeed.
- **To be weak of ears**

  Meaning: To believe everything one hears.
- **To become water water**

  Meaning: To be embarrassed.
- **To chew iron pellets**

  Meaning: To be confronted by an incredibly difficult task.
- **To get results according to actions**

  Meaning: You reap as you sow.
- **To have a mouth like a parrot**

  Meaning: To praise one ownself.
- **To let the donkey graze in the farm, you will not reap fruit nor sin**

  Meaning: Meaningless activity.
- **To light oil lamp full of ghee (clarified butter)**

  Meaning: To rejoice.

- **To make the teeth of enemy sour**
  Meaning: To defeat the enemy.
- **To put an alkaline paste**
  Meaning: To dupe someone.
- **To sprinkle salt on the burn**
  Meaning: To add to the miseries.
- **To talk to the wind**
  Meaning: As fast as the wind.
- **To the end of time**
  Meaning: To the end of time is an extravagant way of saying 'forever'.
- **To wash ones hand in the river**
  Meaning: To be an opportunist.
- **To whiten hair in the sun**
  Meaning: To get experience as age progresses.
- **Toe the line**
  Meaning: If someone toes the line, they follow and respect the rules and regulations.

U

- **Ugly as a stick**
  Meaning: If someone is as ugly as a stick, they are very ugly indeed.
- **Ugly duckling**
  Meaning: An ugly duckling is a child who shows little promise, but who develops later into a real talent or beauty.
- **Uncalled for**
  Meaning: If someone does something bad and unnecessary without consideration for another's feelings, what they do is uncalled for.
- **Under a cloud**
  Meaning: If someone is suspected of having done something wrong, they are under a cloud.

- **Under false colours**

  Meaning: If someone does something under false colours, they pretend to be something they are not in order to deceive people so that they can succeed.
- **Under fire**

  Meaning: If someone is being attacked and cricitised heavily, they are under fire.
- **Under lock and key**

  Meaning: If something is under lock and key, it is stored very securely.
- **Under someone's heel**

  Meaning: If you are under someone's heel, they have complete control over you.
- **Under the gun**

  Meaning: If you're under the gun, you're under pressure to do something.
- **Under the radar**

  Meaning: If something slips under the radar, it isn't detected or noticed.
- **Under the table**

  Meaning: Bribes or illegal payments are often described as money under the table.
- **Under the weather**

  Meaning: If you are feeling a bit ill, sad or lack energy, you are under the weather.
- **Under the wire**

  Meaning: If a person does something under the wire, they do it at the last possible moment.
- **Under your belt**

  Meaning: If you have something under your belt, you have already achieved or experienced it and it will probably be of benefit to you in the future.
- **Under your breath**

  Meaning: If you say something under your breath, you whisper or say it very quietly.

- **Under your nose**

  Meaning: If something happens right in front of you, especially if it is surprising or audacious, it happens under your nose.
- **Under your skin**

  Meaning: If someone gets under your skin, they really annoy you.
- **Under your thumb**

  Meaning: Someone who is manipulated or controlled by another person is under his or her thumb.
- **Uneasy lies the head that wears the crown**

  Meaning: This means that people with serious responsibilities have a heavy burden.
- **Up a gum tree**

  Meaning: If you're up a gum tree, you're in trouble or a big mess.
- **Up a river without a paddle**

  Meaning: If you up a river without a paddle, you are in an unfortunate situation, unprepared and with none of the resources to remedy the matter.
- **Up for grabs**

  Meaning: If something is up for grabs, it is available and whoever is first or is successful will get it.
- **Up in the air**

  Meaning: If a matter is up in the air, no decision has been made and there is uncertainty about it.
- **Up sticks**

  Meaning: If you up sticks, you leave somewhere, usually permanently and without warning– he upped sticks and went to work abroad.
- **Up the spout**

  Meaning: If something has gone up the spout, it has gone wrong or been ruined.
- **Up the wall**

  Meaning: If someone goes up the wall, they get very angry.

- **Up the wooden hill**

  Meaning: When you go up the wooden hill, you go up the stairs to bed.
- **Up to scratch**

  Meaning: If something doesn't come up to scratch, it doesn't meet the standard required or expected.
- **Up to snuff**

  Meaning: If something isn't up to snuff, it doesn't meet the standard expected.
- **Up to speed**

  Meaning: If you bring someone up to speed, you update them on something.
- **Up to your eyes**

  Meaning: When you've got too much work to do, you're up to your eyes in it.
- **Up to your neck**

  Meaning: If someone is very involved in something, they are up to their neck in it, especially if it is something bad or immoral.
- **Up with the lark**

  Meaning: If you get up very early, you're up with the lark.
- **Upper crust**

  Meaning: The upper crust are the upper classes and the establishment.
- **Upper hand**

  Meaning: If you have the upper hand, you have the advantage.
- **Upset the apple cart**

  Meaning: If you upset the apple cart, you cause trouble and upset people.

V

- **Vale of tears**

  Meaning: This vale of tears is the world and the suffering that life brings.

- **Velvet glove**

  Meaning: This idiom is used to describe a person who appears gentle, but is determined and inflexible underneath.

- **Vent your spleen**

  Meaning: If someone vents their spleen, they release all their anger about something.

- **Vicar of Bray**

  Meaning: A person who changes their beliefs and principles to stay popular with people above them is a Vicar of Bray

- **Vicious circle**

  Meaning: A vicious circle is a sequence of events that make each other worse- someone drinks because they are unhappy at work, then loses their job.

- **Virgin territory**

  Meaning: If something is virgin territory, it hasn't been explored before.

- **Volte-face**

  Meaning: If you do a volte-face on something, you make a sudden and complete change in your stance or position over an issue.

- **Vote with your feet**

  Meaning: Disliking of any organization.

- **Void of**

  Meaning: Wanting in destitute of.

- **Vis-a-vis**

  Meaning: In comparison with.

- **Vice-Versa**

  Meaning: An interchange of positions.

- **Vexed question**

  Meaning: Problem that is difficult to solve.

- **Variety in the spice of life**

  Meaning: Variety of different activities, interests, places or people in your life makes it more enjoyable.

- **Variations on the theme of something**
  Meaning: Different ways of doing or saying the same thing.
- **Valley of death**
  Meaning: Death; or a place or period where death is impending.
- **Valley of the shadow of death**
  Meaning: Valleys on earth one must walk through, that is, part of the human experience.
- **Verge on**
  Meaning: To approach or come close to something; to border or be on the edge of something.
- **Vertically challenged**
  Meaning: Of a person, short.
- **Virgin territory**
  Meaning: By extension, ideas or concepts or activities that have not yet been tried, explored or developed.
- **Vote down**
  Meaning: By a majority vote.
- **Vote in**
  Meaning: To collectively approve a nominee into an office or position as a result of voting.
- **Vote out**
  Meaning: To expel the holder of an office or other position through an act of voting.

W

- **Wait for a raindrop in the drought**
  Meaning: When someone is waiting for a raindrop in the drought, they are waiting or hoping for something that is extremely unlikely to happen.
- **Waiting in the wings**
  Meaning: If someone is waiting in the wings, or in the wings, they are in the background, but nearby, ready to act on short notice.
- **Wake up and smell the coffee**
  Meaning: When someone doesn't realise what is really

happening or is not paying enough attention to events around them, you can tell them to wake up and smell the coffee.

- **Wake-up call**

  Meaning: A wake-up call is a warning of a threat or a challenge, especially when it means that people will have to change their behaviour to meet it.
- **Walk a fine line**

  Meaning: If you have to walk a fine line, you have to be very careful not to annoy or anger people or groups that are competing.
- **Walk a mile in my shoes**

  Meaning: This idiom means that you should try to understand someone before criticizing them.
- **Walk in the park**

  Meaning: An undertaking that is easy is a walk in the park. The opposite is also true – "no walk in the park".
- **Walk like an elephant**

  Meaning: No care attitude.
- **Walk on eggshells**

  Meaning: If you have to walk on eggshells when with someone, you have to be very careful because they get angry or offended very easily.
- **Walk the green mile**

  Meaning: Someone or something that is walking the green mile is heading towards the inevitable.
- **Walk the plank**

  Meaning: If someone walks the plank, they are going toward their own destruction or downfall.
- **Walking encyclopaedia**

  Meaning: A very knowledgeable person is a walking encyclopedia.
- **Walking on air**

  Meaning: If you are walking on air, you are so happy that you feel as if you could float.
- **Walking on broken glass**

  Meaning: When a person is punished for something. e.g. 'She had me walking on broken glass.'

- **Walking time-bomb**

  Meaning: A person whose behaviour is erratic and totally unpredictable is a walking time-bomb.

- **War chest**

  Meaning: A war chest is a fund that can be used to finance a campaign like and election or for use in emergencies or unexpected times of difficulty.

- **War of words**

  Meaning: A war of words is a bitter argument between people or organizations, etc.

- **Warm and fuzzy**

  Meaning: The feeling evoked as though you were enclosed in a warm and fuzzy blanket.

- **Warm the cockles of your heart**

  Meaning: If something warms the cockles of your heart, it makes you feel happy.

- **Warpath**

  Meaning: If someone is on the warpath, they are very angry about something and will do anything to get things sorted the way they want.

- **Warts and all**

  Meaning: If you like someone warts and all, you like them with all their faults.

- **Wash your hands of something**

  Meaning: If you wash your hands of something, you disassociate yourself and accept no responsibility for what will happen.

- **Waste not, want not**

  Meaning: If you don't waste things, you are less likely to end up lacking.

- **Waste of skin**

  Meaning: If a person is referred to as a 'waste of skin', it means he is not worth very much.

- **Watch grass grow**

  Meaning: If something is like watching grass grow, it is really boring.

- **Watch your back**

  Meaning: If someone is after your job, or wants to harm you in any way, you need to "watch your back" to metaphorically see what is going on behind you

- **Watch your six**

  Meaning: This idiom means that you should look behind you for dangers coming that you can't see.

- **Water off a duck's back**

  Meaning: If criticism or something similar is like water off a duck's back to somebody, they aren't affected by it in the slightest.

- **Water over the dam**

  Meaning: If something has happened and cannot be changed, it is water over the dam.

- **Water under the bridge**

  Meaning: If something belongs to the past and isn't important or troubling anymore, it is water under the bridge.

- **Watery grave**

  Meaning: If someone has gone to a watery grave, they have drowned.

- **Way to go**

  Meaning: This is used to congratulate someone when they achieve something. It can be used sarcastically when then mess up.

- **Weak at the knees**

  Meaning: If people go weak at the knees, they have a powerful emotional reaction to something and feel that they might fall over.

- **Wear many hats**

  Meaning: If someone wears many hats, they have different roles or tasks to perform.

- **Weasel words**

  Meaning: If somebody uses vague and unspecific terms to try to avoid being clear about their position or opinion, they are using weasel words.

- **Weather a storm**

  Meaning: If you weather a storm, you get through a crisis or hard times.

- **Wee buns**

  Meaning: If a task was wee buns, it means it was very easy. It is similar to "piece of cake".

- **Wee hours**

  Meaning: Wee hours are the first hours after midnight.

- **Well-heeled**

  Meaning: Someone who is well-heeled is rich.

- **Well-oiled**

  Meaning: If someone is well-oiled, they have drunk a lot.

- **Wet cat**

  Meaning: Scared person.

- **What does the blind desires, but of course eyesight**

  Meaning: To desire just the perfect thing.

- **What is the use of repenting now when the bird has eaten the harvest**

  Meaning: No use repenting when it is too late to undo the damage.

- **What you do, so shall you fill**

  Meaning: You will reap as you sow.

- **Writ large**

  Meaning: If something is writ large, it is emphasised or highlighted.

- **Writing on the wall**

  Meaning: If the writing's on the wall for something, it is doomed to fail.

- **Written all over your face**

  Meaning: If someone has done something wrong or secret, but cannot hide it in their expression, it is written all over their face.

- **Written in stone**

  Meaning: If something is written in stone, it is permanent and cannot be changed.
- **Wrong end of the stick**

  Meaning: If someone has got the wrong end of the stick, they have misunderstood what someone has said to them.
- **Wrong foot**

  Meaning: If you start something on the wrong foot, you start badly.
- **Why keep a dog and bark yourself?**

  Meaning: There's no need to do something yourself when you have somebody to do it for you, usually trivial matters.
- **Wide berth**

  Meaning: If you give someone a wide berth, you keep yourself well away from them because they are dangerous.
- **Wide of the mark**

  Meaning: If something is wide of the mark, it is inaccurate or incorrect.
- **Will never fly**

  Meaning: If an idea or project, etc., will never fly, it has no chance of succeeding.
- **Win by a nose**

  Meaning: If somebody wins by a nose, they only just beat the others.
- **Window dressing**

  Meaning: If something is done to pretend to be dealing with an issue or problem, rather than actually dealing with it, it is window dressing.
- **Window to the soul**

  Meaning: Eyes are sometimes referred to as the window to the soul.
- **Winner takes all**

  Meaning: If everything goes to the winner, as in an election, the winner takes all.

- **Wipe the smile of someone's face**

  Meaning: If you wipe the smile of someone's face, you do something to make someone feel less pleased with themselves.

- **With a heavy hand**

  Meaning: If someone does something with a heavy hand, they do it in a strict way, exerting a lot of control.

- **With flying colours**

  Meaning: If you pass something with flying colours, you pass easily, with a very high mark or grade.

- **With friends like that, who needs enemies?**

  Meaning: This expression is used when people behave badly or treat someone badly that they are supposed to be friends with.

- **Wither on the vine**

  Meaning: If something withers on the vine, it fails to get the intended result, doesn't come to fruition.

- **Within a whisker**

  Meaning: If you come within a whisker of doing something, you very nearly manage to do it but don't succeed.

- **Without a hitch**

  Meaning: If something happens without a hitch, nothing at all goes wrong.

- **Wolf in sheep's clothing**

  Meaning: A wolf in sheep's clothing is something dangerous that looks quite safe and innocent.

- **Word of mouth**

  Meaning: If something becomes known by word of mouth, it is because people are talking about it, not through publicity, etc.

- **Words fail me**

  Meaning: If words fail you, you can't find the words to express what you are trying to say.

- **Work like a charm**

  Meaning: If something works like a charm, it works perfectly.

- **Work like a dog**

  Meaning: If you work like a dog, you work very hard.
- **Work the system**

  Meaning: If people work the system, they exploit the state or similar setup to their advantage.
- **World at your feet**

  Meaning: If everything is going well and the future looks full of opportunity, you have the world at your feet.
- **World is your oyster**

  Meaning: When the world is your oyster, you are getting everything you want from life.
- **Worm information**

  Meaning: If you worm information out of somebody, you persuade them to tell you something they wanted to keep from you.
- **Worm's eye view**

  Meaning: A worm's eye view of something is the view from below, either physically or socially.
- **Worth a shot**

  Meaning: If something is worth a shot, it is worth trying as there is some chance of success.
- **Worth your salt**

  Meaning: Someone who is worth their salt deserves respect.

X

- **X factor**

  Meaning: The dangers for people in the military that civilians do not face, for which they receive payment, are known as the X factor.
- **X marks the spot**

  Meaning: This is used to say where something is located or hidden.
- **X-rated**

  Meaning: If something is x-rated, it is not suitable for children.

Y

- **Yank my chain**

  Meaning: If someone says this to another person it means for the other person to leave the person who said it alone and to stop bothering them.

- **Yellow press**

  Meaning: The yellow press is a term for the popular and sensationalist newspapers.

- **Yellow streak**

  Meaning: If someone has a yellow streak, they are cowardly about something.

- **Yellow-bellied**

  Meaning: A yellow-bellied person is a coward.

- **Yen**

  Meaning: If you have a yen to do something, you have a desire to do it.

- **Yes-man**

  Meaning: Someone who always agrees with people in authority is a yes-man.

- **Yesterday's man or Yesterday's woman**

  Meaning: Someone, especially a politician or celebrity, whose career is over or on the decline is yesterday's man or woman.

- **You are what you eat**

  Meaning: This is used to emphasise the importance of a good diet as a key to good health.

- **You can catch more flies with honey than with vinegar**

  Meaning: This means that it is easier to persuade people if you use polite arguments and flattery than if you are confrontational.

- **You can choose your friends, but you can't choose your family**

  Meaning: Some things you can choose, but others you cannot, so you have to try to make the best of what you have where you have no choice.

- **You can lead a horse to water, but you can't make it drink**

  Meaning: This idiom means you can offer something to someone, like good advice, but you cannot make them take it.
- **You can say that again**

  Meaning: If you want to agree strongly with what someone has said, you can say 'You can say that again' as a way of doing so.
- **You can't have cake and the topping, too**

  Meaning: This idiom means that you can't have everything the way you want it, especially if your desires are contradictory.
- **You can't have your cake and eat it**

  Meaning: This idiom means that you can't have things both ways. For example, you can't have very low taxes and a high standard of state care.
- **You can't make a silk purse out of a sow's ear**

  Meaning: If something isn't very good to start with, you can't do much to improve it.
- **You can't make an omelette without breaking eggs**

  Meaning: This idiom means that in order to achieve something or make progress, there are often losers in the process.
- **You can't unring a bell**

  Meaning: This means that once something has been done, you have to live with the consequences as it can't be undone.
- **You could have knocked me down with a feather**

  Meaning: This idiom is used to mean that the person was very shocked or surprised.
- **You do not get a dog and bark yourself**

  Meaning: If there is someone in a lower position who can or should do a task, then you shouldn't do it.
- **You get what you pay for**

  Meaning: Something that is very low in price is not usually of very good quality.

- **You said it!**

  Meaning: Used to say you agree completely with something just said.

- **You scratch my back and I'll scratch yours**

  Meaning: This idiom means that if you do something for me, I'll return the favour.

- **You're toast**

  Meaning: If someone tells you that you are toast, you are in a lot of trouble.

- **You've got rocks in your head**

  Meaning: Someone who has acted with a lack of intelligence has rocks in their head.

- **You've made your bed- you'll have to lie in it**

  Meaning: This means that someone will have to live with the consequences of their own actions.

- **Young blood**

  Meaning: Young people with new ideas and fresh approaches are young blood.

- **Young Turk**

  Meaning: A Young Turk is a young person who is rebellious and difficult to control in a company, team or organization.

- **Your belly button is bigger than your stomach**

  Meaning: If your belly button is bigger than your stomach, you take on more responsibilities than you can handle.

- **Your call**

  Meaning: If something is your call, it is up to you to mak. decision on the matter.

- **You cannot clap with one hand**

  Meaning: It takes two.

- **Your name is mud**

  Meaning: If someone's name is mud, then they have a bad reputation.